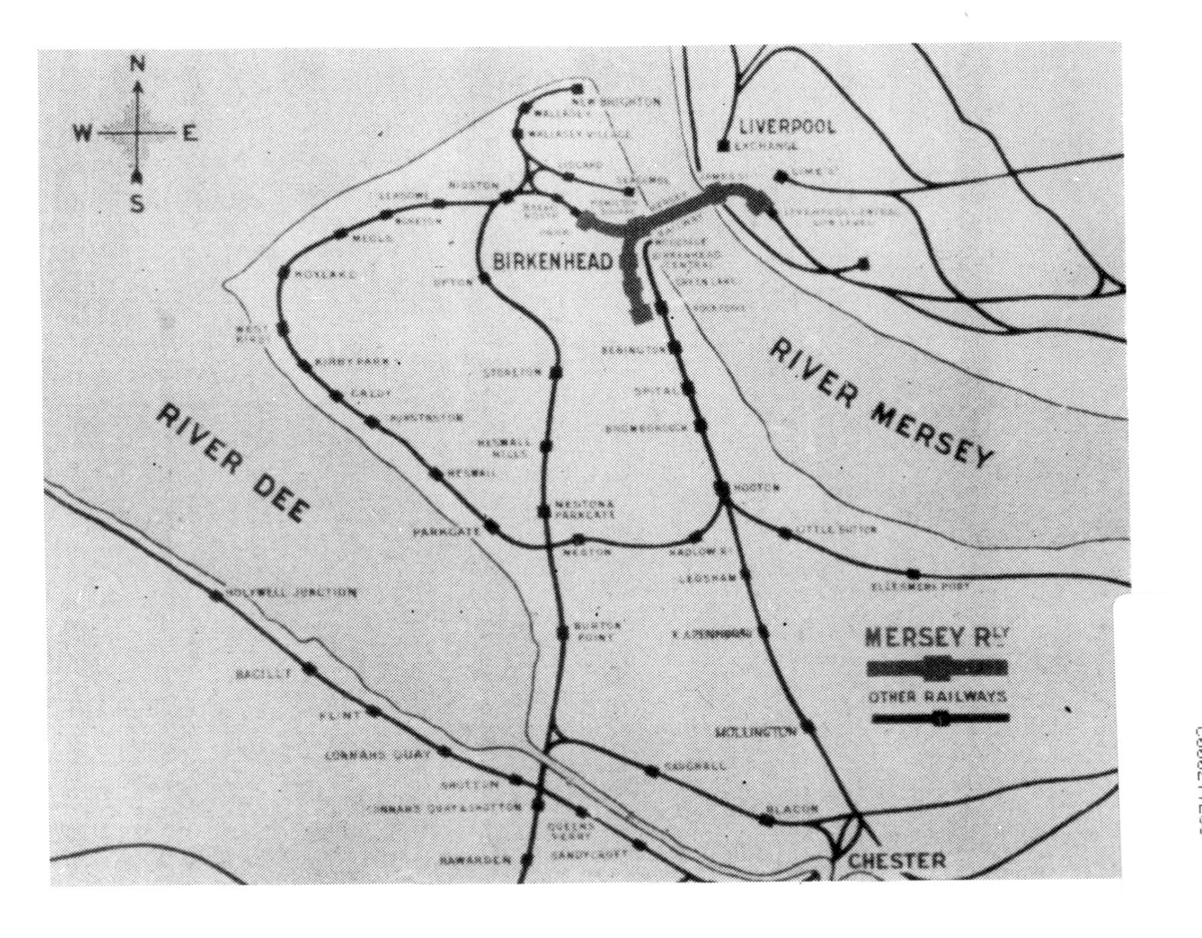
N
W
E
S
LIVERPOOL
BIRKENHEAD
RIVER MERSEY
RIVER DEE
CHESTER
MERSEY R^LY
OTHER RAILWAYS

C000277285

Artist's impression of the opening of the Mersey Railway by the Prince of Wales. (London Illustrated News, 30th January, 1886.)

The Line Beneath The Liners

A hundred years of Mersey Railway sights and sounds

by

John W. Gahan

Cover Design: ERIC R. MONKS.

By the same author:

17 Stations to Dingle — The Liverpool Overhead Railway remembered.

First published 1983 by Countyvise Limited, 1 & 3 Grove Road, Rock Ferry, Birkenhead, Wirral, Merseyside L42 3XS .... ISBN 0 907768 40 7

and

Avon AngliA Publications & Services, Annesley House, 21 Southside, Weston-Super-Mare, Avon BS23 2QU .... ISBN 0 905466 57 8

Photoset and printed by Birkenhead Press Limited, 1 & 3 Grove Road, Rock Ferry, Birkenhead, Wirral, Merseyside, L42 3XS.

FOREWORD

The centenary of the World's first under-river railway will be celebrated in March, 1986. This event will focus attention on a line that has been taken very much for granted over many years, but one that is vital to the thousands of cross-Mersey travellers who use it daily. The Mersey Railway has been an important component of Merseyside's transport facilities for many decades and continues its vital role to this day. Not only was the Mersey Railway the first sub-aqueous line, but it was also the first railway in Britain to be converted from steam to electric traction. This took place as far back as the year 1903, so even as an electric railway it has had a long innings. More important still, it has a future ahead of it.

This book is not a history of the Mersey Railway, even though it contains many historical references. Its main object is to tell the story of the line in non-technical terms and recall the many unique features of this short but busy railway that has been extended in recent times and increased its value to the population on both sides of the river whose name it bears. Readers seeking technical details will find these in other publications. The retrospective and nostalgic aspects have their appeal, and I hope that the book brings pleasure to all who remember the Mersey Railway in its independent days, whilst providing interest for those who travel on it today.

Liverpool,
October, 1982.

MERSEY RAILWAY

TRAINS EVERY FEW MINUTES BETWEEN LIVERPOOL AND BIRKENHEAD

TRAVELLING TIME
From
LIVERPOOL CENTRAL (L.L.)
To
ROCK FERRY - 12 mins.
B'HEAD PARK - 9 mins.
Intermediate Stations proportionately less.

For CHEAP FACILITIES SEE SPECIAL ANNOUNCEMENTS.

MERSEY RAILWAY and its CONNECTIONS.

RIVER MERSEY

RIVER DEE

MERSEY RAILWAY

Through Bookings
and
Frequent Connections
to
CHESTER
and
All Parts of Wirral,
NORTH WALES
CAMBRIAN COAST
MIDLANDS.
All G.W.Rly. Stations,
Etc.

For EXCURSIONS See SPECIAL ANNOUNCEMENTS.

A Mersey Railway advertisement from the year 1926.

Major Isaac's Railway

Liverpool's legendary Liver Bird confronts its citizens boldly, and is probably the symbol by means of which the seaport is best known. It is the most prominent feature of the city's coat-of-arms, which has appeared on trams, buses, municipal vehicles of many other kinds and on a host of civic objects. A stately creature, striding confidently, the giant bird also figured as the centre-piece in the crest of a local railway company — one whose trains were hidden beneath the teeming streets and never saw the light of the city they served so intensively. This was the appropriately-titled Mersey Railway, which provided Liverpool and its neighbour Birkenhead with a remarkably reliable and efficient inter-community passenger train service for the greater part of its 65 years of independent existence. Success did not at first crown its efforts however, as the first 17 years of the railway's life proved difficult and disappointing owing to methods of operation to which there were no reliable alternatives at the time the railway was built.

Whenever the subject of underground railways is discussed, the City of London receives the most attention, somewhat naturally, because the Capital not only possessed the first such railways in Britain, but also a greater mileage of them than any other city in the United Kingdom, of which only two, Liverpool (associated with Birkenhead in this context) and Glasgow eventually had such systems built. The first British underground railways were the Metropolitan and the Metropolitan District, opened in 1863 and 1868 respectively. These were really sub-surface railways which threaded their way below streets in cuttings and tunnels and are quite distinct from the later tube railways which are at deep level and constructed on quite a different principle — their rails run through large diameter steel tubes, although all London Transport lines today are collectively termed the "Underground". A further distinction lies in the fact that the "tubes" have always been electrically operated, which was not the case with the earlier underground systems. Both the Metropolitan and the Metropolitan District Railways were operated for many years with steam locomotives, their trains of plain, austere carriages being hauled by picturesque 4-4-0 Tank locomotives of characteristic "London" design on which the driver and his fireman worked without the shelter of a cab, this refinement not being considered necessary in mid-Victorian days. These locomotives were characterised by their inclined outside cylinders, short-wheelbase leading truck, and prominent condensing pipes, the latter which were provided to convey the exhaust steam to the water tanks in order to avoid having to discharge it into the tunnels. Many of them bore romantic names quite out of keeping with the sulphurous atmosphere in which they worked (and created). Inevitably, electrification was undertaken when this form of traction had become reliably established for intensive train services and among its many benefits was the solution to the extremely severe problem of smoke and fumes in the tunnels, which under steam operation became encrusted with soot. A journey on the London underground lines was considered by many passengers to be a preview of the realm of Satan! Even so, the enginemen who drove and fired these beautiful locomotives survived very well indeed, and many of them, like their machines, enjoyed long, healthy lives. One of the old "Underground" steam locomotives has been retained as a museum-piece, and is now in the London Transport Museum at Covent Garden.

Outside of London, underground railways were hardly contemplated — there was no real need for them in the majority of towns and cities in the British Isles, and it seemed that only London, with its vast size and traffic-congested streets, coupled with a mass passenger transit problem needed railways below the surface. A state of affairs existed on Merseyside in mid-Victorian times however, in which a sub-surface railway offered possibilities, namely the connection of Liverpool and Birkenhead, on opposite shores of the River Mersey. Both places were already linked by old established ferries, which at that time were small paddle steamers, and, good as they were, could provide only a time-consuming journey between the two places. Moreover, the ferries did not land passengers in either town centre, but at wave-lashed stone slipways on the river banks, necessitating a walk or omnibus ride to shops and business premises etc. The river crossing was also subject to the vagaries of the weather — storms and fogs could cause delays or even suspension of the service, and with business in both towns increasing, a better means of communication became vitally necessary.

As far back as the year 1825 proposals were made to tunnel the Mersey but the task seemed almost impossible at the time, and aroused much scepticism. The first serious plans were made in 1864 when railways were well established, in which year the Liverpool & Birkenhead Railway Company was formed and application made to Parliament for Powers to construct a line under the river. The engineers for this project were W.M. Brydone and John Fowler. The railway was planned with its termini to be situated near Brunswick Dock goods depot of the Cheshire Lines system in Liverpool, and a point on the L&NW/GW Joint Chester-Birkenhead railway line between Rock Ferry and New Ferry. At the Liverpool end a branch was intended to connect the railway with the CLC system near St. James's station, whilst on the Cheshire shore two branches were proposed to connect with the Chester—Birkenhead line, at Tranmere and Bebington. The Bill was supported by Ralph Brocklebank, Chairman of the Mersey Docks & Harbour Board, and by W. Hind, who was Chairman of the Birkenhead Commissioners, the governing body of that town. A man whose name is synonimous with Birkenhead, John Laird, MP., also supported the project, as it promised to be of enormous value to the town, which was in the process of expansion. Unfortunately however, the powerful London & North Western Railway Company, which had lines in both Liverpool and Birkenhead and provided a somewhat circuitous route between the two places via Warrington, offered strong opposition and succeeded in defeating the Bill, which was withdrawn in May, 1865, and that, for the time being, was the end of the tunnel scheme.

In the same year that the tunnel Bill was defeated, a scheme for construction of a Mersey bridge was raised. This was planned as a two-deck structure for both rail and road traffic (carts, carriages etc.). The bridge was to commence at the Custom House, Canning Place, Liverpool and terminate near the Birkenhead market and was intended to give a clear headway of 155 feet above high water, two piers to be actually situated in the river. Application was made to Parliament for powers to build the bridge, an action that prompted the tunnel promoters to revive their scheme. Another tunnel project was also raised at the same time by Sir Charles Fox, father of Charles Douglas Fox who became one of the engineers of the subsequently constructed Mersey Railway. To build this latter tunnel and railway, which was to run from the centre of Liverpool to the centre of Birkenhead, the Mersey Pneumatic Railway Company was formed, and as its title implied, it was intended to propel the trains by pneumatic power.

The line was to be a single one only — rather shortsighted in view of the traffic potentialities. The Bill for the Mersey Pneumatic Railway Company was introduced in Parliament by T.B. Horsfall, MP for Liverpool, and John Laird, MP for Birkenhead. The Bill was passed in 1866, that for the bridge being defeated. The Birkenhead Commissioners sought for, and succeeded in obtaining a Compensation Clause in respect of their Mersey Ferry Rights, which was afterwards the cause of much contention between the later Mersey Railway Company and the Corporation of Birkenhead.

The Act permitted construction of an underground railway with its Liverpool terminal situated opposite Compton House, Church Street, that at Birkenhead to be opposite the Woodside Hotel, not far from the ferry landing. Strong efforts were made by the promoters to obtain financial assistance from neighbouring railway companies but without success, and consequent upon the general stagnation in railway promotional activities that followed the financial panic of 1866, the scheme went into abeyance, though the Company held together. Another impediment to the project was the fact that no developments had been made with pneumatic railways, the few built up to that time having been converted to more conventional means of locomotion after various technical troubles had hindered operation.

Other schemes were proposed by other parties about the period under review, but subsequently abandoned. One really optimistic project was that for a tunnel from Bootle to New Brighton, the latter being at that time a small resort which could have provided little traffic. Another more realistic and promising scheme was that for construction of a tunnel between Herculaneum Dock, Liverpool, and Rock Ferry, but this too, came to nothing. On 22nd December, 1869, Sir Charles Fox addressed a well-attended meeting of Liverpool merchants and businessmen, at which he laid before them the manifold advantages of the tunnel railway scheme with which he himself was associated. Present at this meeting were MP's William Rathbone and R.A. Mache, also Robertson Gladstone and Christopher Bushell. The Chairman was John Patterson. At this meeting it was resolved that the pneumatic scheme be dropped and application be made for Powers to substitute a conventional steam operated double-track railway. The Mersey Railway Company was thus formed, and new Powers were applied for during 1870, whilst at the same time Powers for an extension of the line on the Birkenhead side were sought, this to connect with the London & North Western and Great Western Railways.

The Mersey Railway Act was granted in 1871, and shortly afterwards the company made a contract with John Dickson (who had built railways in South Wales and elsewhere) under the terms of which he was required to raise the necessary capital and then construct the railway. Dickson commenced the task by sinking a shaft at Birkenhead, to a depth of about 90 feet which proved the rock to be sound, but unfortunately he encountered financial difficulties so no further work was done and the shaft was abandoned. The company remained in existence however, and awaited a favourable opportunity to make another start. In 1876 they sought the assistance of the Great Western Railway in construction of a station in Paradise Street, Liverpool, without success. Time was passing and little progress was being made and it is possible that the tunnel scheme might not have been heard of again had not a London businessman, Major Samuel Isaac been engaged to carry out the project, which fired his imagination.

Isaac, who was born at Chatham in 1815 became an army contractor with headquarters in Jermyn Street, London, trading as Isaac Campbell & Company. He was a remarkable man, not averse to taking risks, no matter how great and indeed, during the American Civil War the firm's ships, outward bound with army stores for the Confederates and returning with cotton were regular blockade runners. On conclusion of the war the firm suffered financial ruin but Isaac survived this misfortune. He was awarded the military rank of Major due to his activities in forming a regiment of volunteers among the workmen in his factory at Northampton. He eventually became the railway's creator and to him we largely owe the fact of its existence.

Although Major Isaac took a formidable risk in undertaking to complete the tunnel, his problems were physical rather than financial, as he was backed by a number of prosperous men of commerce. In December, 1879 he entered into a preliminary contract with the company to bore a pilot tunnel beneath the Mersey in order to ascertain the nature of the strata through which the main railway tunnel would have to be driven. It was already known that the new red sandstone extended beneath the river bed but the possible existence of faults and quicksands needed to be located before the main task could be put in hand, and in boring the pilot tunnel the ever-present possibility of water cascading into the workings had to be risked. Such an eventuality was, however, provided for by the digging of wells at the shafts, so that in the event of an emergency these would fill up before the tunnel became flooded, thus giving the workmen a chance to get clear.

The contract for the tunnel was sub-let to Messrs. John Waddell & Sons, of Edinburgh, and this company appointed James Brunlees and Charles Douglas Fox as Engineers-in-Chief. In the cold winter weather of December, 1879 hardy workmen broke ground for the shafts in both Liverpool and Birkenhead on land within the boundaries of the Mersey Docks & Harbour Board's territory. The Birkenhead shaft was 17 feet 6 inches in diameter, that at Liverpool having a diameter of 15 feet, each shaft being sunk to a depth of 170 feet. The Liverpool shaft was bored through made-up ground from an early land-winning scheme — consolidated spoil dumped where the river once flowed. It was sunk through the cellars of ancient houses which once stood in long-vanished Bird Street, and during this work several sections of old wooden water pipes were unearthed. Below the old cellars lay the thickness of spoil, then the former river bed, below which came a layer of boulder clay, and finally the sandstone. The distance between the river banks below which the tunnel was to pass was 1,320 yards, the distance between the shafts, which were inland, being 1,770 yards. Other shafts were subsequently sunk for the purpose of bringing spoil to the surface, no less than 24 being bored eventually and sealed up after the work was completed. Boring of the shafts and pilot tunnel was carried out by three shifts of men working eight hours each, the work continuing night and day, but at the request of the Engineers and Contractor, Sunday was strictly a day of rest when no work whatever was done. The Sabbath was widely respected in those mid-Victorian times.

By June, 1881 Major Isaac and his colleagues, being thoroughly satisfied with the work so far accomplished, and after an expenditure of £125,000, felt themselves justified in appealing to the public for further capital. A Board of Directors was formed, the Chairman being the Right Hon. Cecil Raikes M.P. The Vice Chairman was the Right Hon. E.P. Bouverie M.P. K. Boutcher, one of the capitalists who had supported the project since 1879, and George Cavendish Taylor, a director of the London, Chatham & Dover Railway also joined the Board, which was completed by Messrs. G.G. Mott and Alexander Hubbard representing the Great Western Railway. The public response to the appeal for capital was satisfactory, as it was on all subsequent occasions when further capital was needed, and there were no hold-ups on this score. It was decided to commence with the main tunnel before the pilot bore had been completed because no difficulties had been met with, and this task was begun before the end of the year 1881, but it was necessary by that time to apply for Extended Powers.

In October, 1882 the Lord Mayor of London, Sir John Whitaker Ellis, Bart., visited Merseyside and, accompanied by the Mayor of Liverpool, paid a visit to the tunnel works which were the subject of widespread interest at the time. After laying memorial stones in the tunnel, their Worships, together with numerous guests were entertained to luncheon by Major Isaac — but not in an hotel however. Isaac arranged for this function to be held in the tunnel, and as the distinguished company dined in their strange and eerie surroundings the proceedings were enlivened from time to time by the distant rumble of falling rock as blasting proceeded at the heading, the vibration from this activity causing a curious throbbing along the smooth brick arching of the completed portion of the tunnel in which the visitors were assembled, doubtless to their discomfiture!

The work of construction actually involved the boring of three tunnels over much of the distance. The main railway tunnel, which had to be lined with six to eight rings of brickwork and required the immense total of 38,000,000 bricks was bored to a width of 26 feet and a height of 19 feet in order to accommodate the double railway track of standard gauge. Secondly, a ventilation tunnel was required, and thirdly a drainage tunnel, the two latter being merged into one bore for some distance beneath the river. At the centre of the river, lowest point of the tunnel, there is 33 feet of rock between the crown of the arch and the river bed. At James Street and Hamilton Square stations the tunnel was enlarged to a height of 32 feet and span of 50 feet 6 inches. Cross-headings were provided connecting the railway and other tunnels at intervals throughout the under-river section.

Inevitably water was encountered as the work progressed, but strange to relate, it was the landward sections of the tunnel that were the most troublesome in this respect and more so in Liverpool than in Birkenhead. The fact that less water entered the driftway under the river than did under terra-firma was held to be due to the interstices in the rock beneath the river bed being filled with sand and clay, whereas the rock was more broken-up along the banks. In order to keep the workings, and the completed tunnel free from water, continuous pumping was necessary and has remained so since construction days. Ponderous steam pumping machinery was installed in the main working shafts at Liverpool and Birkenhead, the engineers in charge of this section of the undertaking being George Ginty and John Oliver, and they dealt with the problem in a big, and extremely successful manner.

The Liverpool Pumping Station was built adjacent to the now long-vanished Georges Dock, and part of it still stands, looking extremely "early railway" and much repaired following war damage and the ravages of time and weather. It is located at the South-West corner of the intersection of The Strand, James Street and Mann Island (near Canning Dock). Into this tall building, there was installed a pair of pumps with a diameter of 20 inches and stroke of six feet, connected to a Compound steam engine manufactured by Hawthorne Davey & Company of Leeds. This engine featured a differential valve gear by means of which the supply of steam was automatically regulated according to the actual work performed. There were also a pair of pumps 30 inches in diameter, 15 feet stroke, also driven by a Hawthorne Davey engine. The largest installation here however, was a massive steam beam engine built by Andrew Barclay & Sons, of Kilmarnock, which actuated two pumps 40 inches in diameter, with a stroke of 15 feet. The balance beam of this colossal engine measured 19 feet in length from its rocking centre to the centre of the pump rods and 24 feet 6 inches long from the rocking centre to the end. The main beam was composed of two plates and measured 32 feet 6 inches between extreme centres. The connecting rod was no less than 38 feet 9 inches in length! The machinery installed at Shore Road, Birkenhead, was similar but there were two Barclay 40-inch pumps with a stroke of 15 feet driven by steam beam engines and one 30-inch pump driven by a Hawthorne Davey engine. Arrangements were made by which water from both sides of the river could be collected at either pumping station so that engines could be shut down for any repairs or other attention that might be required. The immense quantities of water which a single pump could deal with was exemplified by the fact that the 40-inch Liverpool pump could, with four-and-a-half strokes, raise 3,672 gallons; the smaller 30-inch pumps could each raise about the same amount with six strokes. Water raised at the Liverpool end of the tunnel was emptied into Georges Dock passage, which was adjacent to the pumping station.

The pumping plant was capable of dealing with four-times the amount of water that entered the drainage tunnels so that there was an ample safety margin in the event of a failure. In fact, about four hours would have elapsed before the water reached rail level. (The safety margin today is even greater with electrical pumps at work and less water penetrating into the drainage tunnels than was the case in earlier years).

The progress of the tunnelling works was followed with considerable interest both in and outside the Merseyside area. On 12th October, 1883, Mr. and Mrs. Gladstone visited the workings accompanied by Lord and Lady Derby, Sir John Lubbock and Lady Margaret Cecil. Gladstone was a firm supporter of the tunnel scheme and also of the mooted construction of a railway below the broad estuary of the River Dee to North Wales, which however, was not proceeded with, being a little too ambitious and costly to tackle. To-day, almost a century later there is still talk of tunnelling or bridging the Dee, but not for the passage of trains, alas.

By the beginning of 1884 1,400 men and 177 horses toiled in the depths on the work of construction which was pushed ahead vigorously. The original plan for the land sections was to employ the cut-and-cover method of construction whereby the streets would be excavated to the required depth, then the resultant cutting roofed over and the streets remade. Fierce opposition from traders as well as owners and occupiers of buildings forced the company to abandon this plan and bore the tunnel instead. There was a certain amount of trouble on the Birkenhead side due to sinking and damage to buildings in Hamilton Street while the tunnel was under construction, which made the project quite unpopular for a while! A small amount of cut-and-cover construction was however, carried out in Birkenhead, notably where the Mersey line passes under the docks branch of the Birkenhead—Chester main line near the Haymarket. Initially the tunnelling was carried out by manual work, the time-honoured picks and shovels being used, together with explosives. Dynamite was tried at first but discarded due to the noxious fumes produced and Gelignite substituted. In February, 1883 a compressed air boring machine, invented by Colonel Beaumont of the Royal Engineers was introduced on the Birkenhead side and this was capable of boring about 17 yards per week — manual excavation averaged 10—13 yards per week. Thus the work went steadily on with no set-backs of any consequence and at a satisfactory rate. Indeed, the men worked by electric light which greatly facilitated the task, and it seems odd in view of this up-to-date illumination that the completed tunnel and stations were lit by gas, the latter deemed to be more reliable at that early date.

On 17th January, 1884 the two headings met beneath the bed of the River Mersey at a point 1,115 yards from the Birkenhead working shaft. The last few feet of rock were cleared away in the presence of the Chairman, the Right Hon. Cecil Raikes M.P. Also present were Major Isaac, Colonel Beaumont, Messrs. Brunlees, Fox, Patterson (Mayor of Birkenhead), D. Ratcliffe (Mayor of Liverpool) and a number of other interested persons. After exchanging congratulations the Liverpool party, headed by the Chairman struggled through the narrow gap past the boring machine to join the men who had worked from the Birkenhead side, and thus became the first of many millions to pass beneath the River Mersey, instead of sailing across as so many generations had before them.

The two tunnels were joined with remarkable accuracy, their centres being less than one inch from each other — an excellent feat of engineering skill when the conditions under which the work had to be carried out are considered. Neither of the shafts at Liverpool and Birkenhead was in the centre line of the railway, and the greatest length of base line that could be secured from which to work was 12 feet. The distance across from shaft to shaft was 1,770 yards, or a little more than one mile.

The railway tunnel slopes downwards from both banks to its lowest point at the centre of the river, but the drainage tunnels were arranged to slope the opposite way so that the water which constantly penetrates the tunnel drains towards the banks to be then dealt with by the pumps. The railway tunnel was lined with six-to-eight rings of brickwork set into cement, the two inner courses consisting of either blue Staffordshire or

Buckley bricks. Incidentally, the making and transportation of these were immense tasks in themselves, 38 million being quite a formidable amount. Considering the conditions and complexity of the construction the perfection of the finished work was remarkable.

The immense task of tunnelling the river, together with the laying and equipping of the railway was completed towards the close of the year 1885 and preparations were made for the opening ceremony. Before the railway was opened for regular traffic the public were permitted to walk through the gaslit tunnel, many thousands taking the opportunity of this preview. The precedent for this subsequent custom originated with the Wapping Tunnel of 1829 and was repeated 49 years after the Mersey Railway tunnel was completed when the road tunnel was finished in 1934. Likewise, the public were allowed to walk through the newer Wallasey road tunnel built subsequently.

On 4th January, 1886 General Hutchinson carried out the Board of Trade inspection and was entirely satisfied. His report was completed with the following words of praise: "In conclusion I think it only just to remark that great credit appears to be due to the engineer and contractors who have so ably carried out and brought to so satisfactory a conclusion this great and important work".

The opening of the railway was the occasion of a Royal visit. H.R.H. The Prince of Wales had consented to perform the ceremony, which took place on Wednesday 20th January, 1886, a bitterly cold day with snow on the ground and an East wind sweeping through the streets to chill the waiting crowds. Thousands of spectators turned out in spite of the weather and all admired the lavish decorations on buildings both in Liverpool and Birkenhead, and of course, on the railway's stations. The Prince of Wales, accompanied by Prince Albert Victor and Prince Edward George, all three of whom had spent the night at Eaton Hall, boarded the Royal train at Chester which, hauled by a Great Western Railway locomotive departed at 11.0 a.m. At Union Street, near Rock Ferry, Mersey Railway locomotive No.2 "Earl of Chester" took over the train and gained Mersey metals by means of a temporary connection from the main line. The train passed through the gaily decorated Green Lane station at 12.0 noon, and a few minutes later drew to a halt at Birkenhead Central station, where the Prince was met by the Mayor and Corporation of that town, also directors of the Mersey Railway. Shortly afterwards the train proceeded to Hamilton Square where the Royal party detrained and spent some time at the pumping station and in viewing other items of interest. The streets surrounding the station were thronged with spectators determined not to miss a single episode in the proceedings.

After re-boarding the train, the trip beneath the Mersey to Liverpool was soon accomplished. Arrival at James Street was greeted by further enthusiastic spectators who packed the streets in the station area. Emerging from the precincts of the station the Royal visitors were met by the Lord Mayor, David Radcliffe J.P., the Lord Lieutenant of the County and Lady Sefton, Lord Claude and Lady Hamilton and other notable persons. As the time fixed for the opening ceremony drew near, the wintry sun emerged from the low cloud and mist to shed its mellow light over Merseyside and lift the hearts of all who were present on this historic occasion. The scene was one of colour and pageantry with the decorations, the crowds, and the uniforms of the Guard of Honour provided by soldiers from Seaforth Barracks, and everything went smoothly as planned.

At precisely one o'clock in the afternoon, the Prince, watched by a suddenly silent crowd, stepped onto a specially prepared dais in James Street and innaugurated the railway with the terse proclamation thus — "I declare the Mersey Railway now open". The long dream of a sub-Mersey railway was a reality at last. The Royal party and their entourage, together with the distinguished visitors next proceeded to the Town Hall for dinner and speeches.

The Mersey Railway was opened for public traffic ten days later, on Monday 1st February, in the chilly dawn of which the first regular train left Green Lane for Liverpool at 4.45. A ten-minute service began at 8 o'clock. An estimated total of 36,000 passengers travelled on the trains on the first day of service, this enormous number being handled successfully, probably due to the fact that all through the previous week trains had been operated in order to test the feasibility of the schedules and to familiarise the staff with their duties. The only hitch on the first day was the stalling of a train in mid-river, which caused a short delay, otherwise everything went smoothly. Approximate passenger totals for the rest of the week were as follows: Tuesday 27,000; Wednesday 22,000; Thursday 22,000; Friday 22,000; Saturday 23,000; Sunday 25,000. The railway had its first taste of heavy holiday traffic on Easter Monday, 26th April, 1886, a clear sunny day on which 50,000 or so people travelled on the trains, a fact which amply demonstrated the capacity of the line. On this Bank Holiday the river ferries did better however, for they handled 53,000 passengers, but of course, there were several ferry services and also, they served the seaside resort of New Brighton, whereas the railway was purely a town to town facility for business traffic, although it gave access to the Wirral countryside, for those who enjoyed long walks.

The construction of the Mersey Railway was a notable engineering triumph that has never received the recognition it deserves, due mainly perhaps to the fact that it is out of sight to all but actual passengers. The Mersey road tunnel opened in 1934 is hailed as one of the wonders of the world, and notable though it is, was completed 49 years after the railway tunnel, advanced machinery being available on the project which the men who bored the railway tunnel did not have at their disposal. The fact that the Mersey Railway tunnel was built so long ago escapes the notice of most of the citizens — the illuminated and extremely prominent portals of the road tunnel being much more in the public vision. However, after only 35 years of service the road tunnel had outgrown its capacity and another one has had to be built, but the railway has been able to absorb increasing passenger loadings with little difficulty, due to the vast superiority of the rail principal where mass transit is concerned — a fact now recognised and being acted upon in many cities where it has long been ignored. The capacity of the original Mersey Railway has been vastly increased with relatively minor alterations and an extension within Liverpool, of which more later.

Construction of the Mersey Railway proved to be Major Isaac's last "battle", as unfortunately he did not live for long after its opening. He was however; spared the anguish of witnessing the difficulties and near ruin that lay ahead. Isaac died at Maida Vale, London on 22nd November, 1886.

As first constructed, the Mersey Railway extended from James Street, Liverpool to Green Lane, Birkenhead, with intermediate stations at Hamilton Square (deep level), and a near street-level station in the town (Birkenhead Central). At the latter station the railway emerges into the open and passes through a cutting, entering another tunnel for the remainder of its course to Green Lane Station, which is just below street level in the district of Tranmere and is situated nearby the Mersey shipbuilding yards, which were well established when the railway was opened. In 1884 Parliamentary sanction was given for a branch line from Hamilton Square to Birkenhead Park, mostly in tunnel. This branch was opened on 2nd January, 1888. At "Park", as the station has always been known, the Mersey Railway metals met those of the Seacombe, Hoylake & Deeside (later Wirral) Railway, which was extended from its former terminus at Birkenhead Docks to meet it, thus through-carriage working was established, passengers being able to travel from Liverpool to Hoylake without change of train, only the locomotives being changed. This through working was later abolished and "Park" became an interchange station. The Mersey line emerges into the open a little way short of the station platforms.

On 16th June, 1891 an extension was opened from Green Lane to Rock Ferry. The tunnel proper ends at Green Lane, the line then climbing a steep gradient in a cutting which becomes progressively shallower and emerges onto an embankment to run parallel, for some distance with the Birkenhead—Chester main line, which was operated jointly by the London & North Western and Great Western companies who also owned this last stretch of "Mersey" line. Also in 1891, the tunnel on the Liverpool side of the river was extended below the city streets to the Central Station of the Cheshire Lines Railway, terminating below it in what is still known today as Central Low Level station. The course of the tunnel is exactly beneath Lord and Church Streets in the shopping centre of the city. This useful extension on a gradient of 1 in 31-34, was opened to traffic on 11th January, 1892. An earlier scheme had been to extend the line to connect with the CLC system near Parliament

Street, but this was not carried out until the Merseyrail project of the 1970's.

The lengths of the tunnel sections of the Mersey Railway are as follows: Liverpool Central to Birkenhead Hamilton Square 1 mile 1,430 yards; Hamilton Square to Birkenhead Park 1,633 yards; Hamilton Square to Birkenhead Central 754 yards. There is no break in the tunnel at Hamilton Square, daylight being encountered for the first time at Birkenhead Central on the Rock Ferry line and at Birkenhead Park on the branch that connects with the former Wirral company's lines.

Liverpool (James Street) and Birkenhead (Hamilton Square) stations, with their platforms at deep level, had to be provided with lifts, and these, like everything else on the Mersey Railway were built on the grand scale. The hydraulic lifts, installed by Messrs. Easton & Anderson, were each operated by a massive direct-acting ram which pushed the lift upwards or lowered it safely down. The installation of these lifts required the excavation in the solid sandstone, of wells 90 feet deep and 40 inches in diameter for the cylinders. Messrs. Mather & Platt, of Salford carried out the work at James Street with a boring machine; Messrs. Timmins, of Runcorn undertook the similar job at Hamilton Square.

Three lifts were provided at each station. The cars were built by the Starbuck Carriage & Wagon Company of Birkenhead, although they bore the brass plates of Easton & Anderson, and each was of such an immense size that they became known as "flying ballrooms"! Each lift (which accommodated 100 passengers) measured 20 feet in length, 17 feet in width and 8 feet 10 inches in height. Longitudinal tram-type wooden seats were provided along each side. The speed of these gigantic lifts was 120 feet per minute — a dignified glide, the journey time between street and lower level and vice-versa taking 45 seconds, so that a total of 300 passengers could be cleared in one minute. A liftman rode in each car and manipulated the control ropes and gates. These ponderous be-panneled and ornate lifts were illuminated by gas lamps, the light being reflected by mirrors in the raised clerestory.

The hydraulic towers, at the tops of which the water tanks were installed were 120 feet in height above street level, and were the most prominent feature of each station. The James Street tower was destroyed during an air raid in May, 1941, but that at Hamilton Square still stands, a fascinating and good-looking example of Victorian railway architecture. A modern touch is imparted to the tower by coloured neon signs, which after darkness has fallen pin-point the station and advertise the train service. The hydraulic lift plant consisted of three marine-type boilers at James Street, Liverpool and two land-type boilers at Birkenhead, Hamilton Square. At James Street there were three steam pumping engines, each capable of raising 30,000 gallons of water per hour from the underground tank to that at the top of the tower. Similar engines performed the same task at Hamilton Square.

Before the hydraulic lifts were put into service they were inspected and rigorously tested by General Hutchinson of the Royal Engineers, on behalf of the Board of Trade. For the test each lift was loaded to 50 percent more than its rated capacity, and not only were weights placed evenly on the floors but the lifts were tried with uneven loads with weights to one side. These severe tests were passed with complete success and amply demonstrated the immense margin of safety available against overloading.

In addition to the lifts, Hamilton Square and James Street stations have flights of steps. At the latter, a lengthy pedestrian subway was constructed to give access to Water Street, opened on 21st April, 1886. This subway, like the lifts and stations was illuminated by gas lamps. Still in use, it imposes a tiring strain on persons walking from station to street due to the upward slope, but in the opposite direction it induces plenty of acceleration! Nevertheless, generations of passengers have cursed the subway and few people use it in the upward direction unless they have to! James Street was of course, a terminus for six years, so a short extension had to be provided for shunting purposes.

The original Mersey Railway permanent-way consisted of bull-head type rails which weighed 85 pounds per yard, joined by deep fishplates and laid in chairs weighing 54 pounds each. The rails were laid on wooden cushions recessed into the chairs, which in turn were laid on timber sleepers measuring 10 feet by 5 inches. Two thicknesses of felt were inserted below each chair. The sleepers, placed closer together than in normal railway practice rested on ballast, consisting of a base of broken sandstone from the tunnel works with a 6 inches thick top layer of clinker.

The Mersey system became permanently connected to the main Birkenhead—Chester line in March, 1886 when a crossover was laid at Union Street, Birkenhead (replacing the temporary connection over which the Royal train had passed on the opening day) and a signal box containing 20 levers was built. The connection has never seen heavy usage, being intended mainly for the interchange of rolling stock, mainly goods wagons containing supplies for railway purposes, stores, engineering equipment etc. The railway remained physically isolated from any other at Liverpool until the new works of the 1970's, of which more later.

When the Mersey Railway was first opened the Third class single fare between James Street and Hamilton Square was three-halfpence, the return fare being twopence-halfpenny. The opening was not viewed favourably among shopkeepers and traders in Birkenhead, who feared that Liverpool would get much of their business, and they were correct to some extent because the town did lose some trade. Business was poor throughout the country in 1886, the situation being so bad that unemployed persons rioted in Trafalgar Square, London, but in Birkenhead all ills were blamed on "The Tunnel" or "sewer" as it was often referred to. Generally however, the line was popular for the frequent and rapid services it provided, but this popularity was destined to decrease fairly soon.

The new railway embarked on its career full of hope for a prosperous future but the odds against this were very great. Steam operation posed ventilation problems that required expensive plant, water seepage necessitated continuous pumping, stations required lifts and lighting. None of these made money — they merely devoured the profits and it was not very long before the company fell on evil days. Revenue decreased year by year until the black year of 1902 when working expenses were in excess of receipts by over £4,000. Indeed only two years or so after the opening, the railway was placed in the hands of a receiver on the orders of the Court of Chancery.

Owing to the fact that the tunnel became increasingly smoke-laden as the working day progressed, the public became discouraged from travelling on the trains and reverted to the ferry steamers in ever-increasing numbers, thus railway revenue steadily declined. Although the ferries were slow in operation they at least provided a fresh-air trip which was preferable to the train in the particular circumstances. The presence of smoke in the tunnels was an insuperable problem even though a ventilation tunnel was provided and in addition giant steam-driven Guibal fans whirled continuously in an effort to clear the atmosphere. These could not deal adequately with the problem however, and in any case were not an asset to the company, being strictly non-revenue equipment which only increased the financial burden.

The ventilating fans were driven by horizontal steam engines — four in number, each dealing with a particular section of tunnel. Two were installed at Liverpool (James Street), one of 40-feet diameter, the other with a diameter of 30-feet. A 40-foot fan was installed at Shore Road, Birkenhead and a 30-foot fan was provided on the North side of Hamilton Street midway between Hamilton Square and Central stations. (The old red-brick fan house with its castellated tower still stands in Hamilton Street, now occupied by a firm of sign makers). The width of each fan was 12 feet. All four fans, when working together, delivered 600,000 cubic feet of air per minute, which was intended to effect a complete change of atmosphere every seven minutes. An early improvement made to the fans was the fitting of an A-shaped regulating shutter by means of which the air passed into the chimney in a continuous current rather than intermittently as was the case when they were first installed, thus rendering the operation noiseless. All four fans and their engines were provided by Walker Brothers of Pagefield Ironworks, Wigan. They must have presented an awe-inspiring sight when in operation, but one that gave no joy to the anxious directors!

An enterprising firm opened two refreshment rooms on the Mersey Railway — one at James Street, the other at Hamilton Square. Owing to the forbidding atmosphere however, the staff turnover was continuous and eventually staff could not be obtained at all, so the rooms were closed, never to be re-opened. Present day passengers will be interested to hear that James Street station featured a fireplace in the upper hall by which passengers warmed themselves in the winter months, preferring to stay off the platforms until almost train time. This fireplace was boarded over after 1903 but was "discovered" during alterations being made to the concourse about 1935.

A Mersey Railway sign from James Street station. (Photo: H. Haddrill.)

Rear view of the old Mersey Railway Fan House in Hamilton Street, Birkenhead. October, 1982. This building contained the fan which dealt with the Hamilton Square – Birkenhead Central section of the tunnel. (Photo: G. Jones.)

Power for the Grades — The Steam Locomotives

The Mersey Railway is neither straight nor level throughout its length. The tunnel section inclines steeply towards the centre of the river on a slope of 1 in 27 from Liverpool and 1 in 30 from Birkenhead, and a stud of extremely powerful locomotives was required to work the frequent train service. The classical "London" type of 4-4-0 Tank locomotive with large coupled wheels was not suitable for the Mersey Railway owing to the steep gradients, therefore a series of 0-6-4 Tank engines with inside cylinders and outside frames was built by Beyer, Peacock & Company of Manchester. These were not only the first engines of this wheel arrangement in Britain, but were also the most powerful Tank locomotives built up to that time. They were followed by some outside-cylindered 2-6-2 Tank engines from the same manufacturer and several from Kitson & Company of Leeds. These locomotives had no cabs, their footplates being completely uncovered, though weather shields were provided fore and aft, but as the bulk of the running was in tunnels the absence of weather protection was not of such great consequence. Both locomotive types were equipped with condensing apparatus which was designed to divert the exhaust steam into the water tanks, but this apparatus was not entirely effective, hence the tunnel ventilation problem.

The steam locomotive fleet consisted of eight 0-6-4 Tank engines by Beyer, Peacock & Company, built 1885-6 and ten of the 2-6-2 Tank type, built 1886-7. The 0-6-4's were numbered and named as follows:—

1. "The Major"
2. "Earl of Chester"
3. "Duke of Lancaster"
4. "Gladstone"
5. "Cecil Raikes"
6. "Fox"
7. "Liverpool"
8. "Birkenhead"

These machines, Mersey Railway Class 1, had cylinders measuring 21 x 23 inches, coupled wheels 4 ft 7 inches in diameter, and a working pressure of 150 lbs per square inch. Tank capacity was 1,250 gallons of water. Weight in working order amounted to 67 tons 17 cwt.

The 2-6-2 Tank engines, Mersey Railway Class 2 and Class 3 carried the following numbers and names:—

9. "Connaught"
10. "Mersey"
11 "Victoria"
12. "Bouverie"
13. "Brunlees"
14. "Tranmere"

15 "Salisbury"
16. "Burcot"
17. "Burnley"
18. "Banstead"

Leading particulars of the 2-6-2 locomotives were as follows:— cylinders 19 x 26 inches; coupled wheels 4 ft 7 inches in diameter; working pressure 150 lbs per square inch; tank capacity 1,150 gallons of water. Weight in working order was 62½ tons for Class 2 and 67 tons 9 cwt for class 3. Both classes were outwardly similar. Engines numbered 9—15 were by Beyer, Peacock & Company, the remainder were the Kitson engines.

The Mersey Railway locomotives were well maintained and cared-for and presented a resplendent sight with their dark-green boiler and tanks with contrasting brown wheels and frames. It was the age of spit and polish on the railways, and though the Mersey locomotives might work amid soot and grime of their own making, they were polished until they positively gleamed.

The engine crews on the Mersey Railway were busy men. Not only did they have to drive and fire, but they had to couple and uncouple from trains numerous times in the course of a day's work. In addition, the condensing apparatus heated the water in the tanks and these had to be emptied at Liverpool Central and re-filled with cold water after every trip, otherwise the steam would not condense. Fires had also to be cleaned and coal taken on. The discharge of hot water in the station area at Liverpool Central necessitated the installation of a 12-foot diameter Guibal fan, driven by a compound steam engine in order to disperse the clouds of steam and engine smoke because this operation was carried out beyond the platform well out of reach of the main fan at James Street. When a train arrived at Central, the engine was detached and drew ahead into the tunnel where the electric trains went in later days (although it was a shorter tunnel then) for discharge of water and re-filling, the train being taken out by the engine from the previous one which was waiting on the engine loop, having been through the servicing ritual, and the process was repeated all day. The engine shed was at Birkenhead Central.

It is of interest to note that although all the large fans were removed after the railway had been electrified, the small fan at Liverpool Central remained, almost forgotten for about 70 years, being finally disposed of when drastic alterations to the station were made in the early 1970's, of which more later. The old fan was extensively corroded after so many years of disuse. Its motive power had long since gone however.

Steam Era Rolling Stock

The Mersey Railway passenger rolling stock in the steam era consisted of 97 four-wheeled compartment type carriages with almost flat roofs, and each close-coupled train consisted of eight vehicles (two First Class, two Second Class and four Third Class carriages). Most of the carriages were of one particular class but there were a few composite examples, whilst many had sections for the guard and luggage. There was also one complete guard's van with no passenger accommodation. Every vehicle was 27 feet in length and eight feet wide, with a wheelbase of 15 feet, six inches. All the vehicles were built by the Ashbury Carriage & Iron Company. Illumination was by gas, on Pintch's system, the gas being produced by the railway company in its own small works situated at Birkenhead Central station. The majority of the carriages were built in 1885 but additions were made in 1887 and 1891. The vacuum brake was employed instead of the Westinghouse air brake more common on lines with intensive train services stopping at closely spaced stations. A peculiar feature of the numbering system was that each class of carriage was numbered from 1 upwards resulting in many examples of two or even three carriages bearing the same fleet number!

It was a full-time task trying to keep the fleet of passenger carriages clean, due to the smoke and soot-laden atmosphere in the tunnels. The upholstery suffered badly, and when the time came to dispose of the vehicles the upholstery was taken out and burned, being unfit for any further use. Cleaners with mops and buckets were employed at the open-air stations of Rock Ferry and Birkenhead Park to give the trains a wash, and they seem to have done a creditable job.

The riding qualities of the short wheelbase "four-wheelers" was anything but smooth, whilst packed compartments in rush hours were the ultimate in discomfort. However, journeys were of short duration so passengers did not spend more than a few minutes in the trains, for which no doubt, they were extremely thankful.

Locomotive No.12 "Bouverie". This went to the Alexandra Docks and Railway, in South Wales for use on coal trains. (Photo: J.W. Gahan.)

Mersey Railway locomotive No.1 "The Major". This went to Australia and is now (1982) undergoing restoration to its original condition. (Photo: K. Longbottom collection.)

The former Mersey Railway locomotive "Cecil Raikes", looking extremely woebegone after a long period of outdoor storage. Photographed at Kirkby Industrial estate on arrival from Derby in 1965. The locomotive later went to the Liverpool City Engineer's Depot at Breckside Park for restoration, but little work was carried out and it is now at Steamport Transport Museum, Southport (1982). (Photo: Merseyside County Museums.)

Mersey Railway No.5 "Cecil Raikes" awaiting restoration at the Southport "Steamport" museum. The engine is in a partially dismantled condition. (Photo: G. Jones.)

Surviving building (pump house) of the former complex of engine and Boiler Houses at Mann Island, Liverpool. October, 1982. The lighter brickwork indicates where a former building adjoined. (Photo: G. Jones.)

The Daily Scene in the Days of Steam

There are probably few persons still around who can recall a trip on the Mersey Railway in the now remote era when the line was steam operated, and what a complete contrast from today was the scene presented before the gaze of the passenger of the 1890's. Few mechanically propelled vehicles had as yet appeared on the streets, so approach to the railway would be made by carriage or Hansome cab by the well-to-do, whilst humbler persons travelled in horse-drawn trams and omnibuses. These picturesque vehicles shared the paved or cobblestoned streets with carts and lorries, with their multifarious loads of merchandise, trundling slowly along behind plodding teams of horses. Liverpool was throwing off the squalor of earlier years and expanding at a fast rate and Birkenhead was also in the throes of expansion but not alas, into the "grand city of the future", which was the dream of its founders back in the 1840's. The Mersey Railway was to be the means of furthering the commercial progress of both towns despite its initial shortcomings.

In the 1880's, as today, the scene at the Mersey Railway stations was one of constant movement of people, although the pace was slower than it is nowadays, and a mixed variety of passengers travelled to and fro on business and pleasure. The dress of the period posed a few problems on a constantly crowded railway like the Mersey on which passengers filled the trains to capacity, in narrow compartments with little room. The business-men, wearing top hats or bowlers travelled First Class, whilst the "artisans and labourers", to quote the Victorian reference to workmen travelled Third Class. Ladies, in their flouncy skirts with floor-level hemlines and bustles had quite a problem in such travelling conditions, and perforce acquired much skill in deftly manoeuvring themselves into and out of the trains, whilst the large hats of the period added to the problems. Rush periods were best avoided by lady passengers because of the crush, especially when the dock and shipyard men beseiged the trains, crowding in and adding pungent tobacco smoke to the already foul and sulphurous atmosphere!

Passengers descending in the huge hydraulic lifts inhaled the products of combustion from the locomotive's fireboxes as they emerged onto the murky platforms — a constant haze that the constantly revolving fans could not entirely clear. Trains were frequent so that nobody had long to wait, which was fortunate. The station staff at places like James Street and Hamilton Square were of necessity, hardy types, as hours of work were long on the railways, as they also were in most other industries, and a long day of inhaling smoke in the subterranean depths was not the most pleasant of occupations. How they must have envied their colleagues at stations like Birkenhead Central and Birkenhead Park with their platforms in the open air

When a train drew into a station passengers stood clear to avoid the dozens of opening doors, then when it halted, made for the compartments appropriate to their class and squeezed in whilst the porters followed up slamming the carriage doors. The "right-away" was quickly given and the train was soon on the move again, plunging into the tunnel and accelerating rapidly, the small coupled wheels of the locomotive revolving at a furious pace and the coupling rods and cranks flailing in a whirl, whilst the exhaust blast was of such violence as to cause the carriage windows to rattle! Passengers inside the confined compartments (and engine crews!) were warned of the approach of a station by "rail clangers" — devices actuated by the wheels, which sounded like exploding detonators. Upon hearing these the more impatient passengers leapt to their feet, grabbed the door handles and swung the doors open before the train stopped, after which they would leap out and make a dash for the lift — a practice that continued with the electric trains after conductors (whom were employed on the latter) had been eliminated, of which more later.

When a train departed from Liverpool James Street for Birkenhead, or from the latter place for Liverpool, the locomotive was driven flat-out on full regulator down the gradient towards the centre of the river in order to gain plenty of momentum to assault the upward gradient, which slowed each train to such an extent that it would enter the next station with the engine still working steam. In the narrow compartments of the four-wheeled carriages the passengers sat, and in rush hours stood also, in the gaslight and inhaled the smoke and fumes that entered through the ventilators. Few people used the line as a matter of choice; those with time to spare preferred the ferries except when the river was rough or when fog affected river traffic.

Electrification

As events turned out, the Mersey Railway proved to have been built just a few years too soon, for a revolution in railway motive power made its appearance in the early 1890's and Liverpool was to be in the van of progress in this respect. In 1893 the Liverpool Overhead Railway, serving the dock estate was opened and, being operated by electric power showed just how effective this new medium was for intensive train services. In London also, the City & South London Railway was being electrically worked with success. The directors of the struggling Mersey Railway did not view the shortcomings of their own line with equanimity — they were fully alive to the potential benefits of electrification but alas, there was no money available and steam operation had to continue for another decade of worsening finances and depleted traffic. In 1896 the company optimistically applied for Parliamentary Powers to enable them to electrify and these were granted, but the conversion could not at that time be implemented.

By the late 1890's the outlook for the Mersey Railway was bleak indeed. The financial position got steadily worse and there was no hope of recovery while existing methods of operation prevailed. Fortunately however, rescue was at hand — from the United States of America, in the person of George Westinghouse, a famous name in railway annals. Westinghouse, an engineer and inventor arrived in England in 1899 to found a business, the British Westinghouse Electric & Manufacturing Company which he established at Trafford Park near Manchester. An advocate of railway electrification of which he had considerable experience in his native land, his attention soon focussed on the Mersey Railway, and on giving the system the "once over" soon drew up an estimate for conversion which he put before the harrassed directors. Again the old problem of finance arose but Westinghouse offered to put money into the coffers and carry out the electrification work, which would give his new business a flying start. Meanwhile electrification of street tramways became the latest thing — all over the country the tram horses were being retired and copper wires on their ornamental standards were giving city streets an air of efficiency whilst the new and magnificent "electric cars" glided along their shining rails. Liverpool tramways were in course of electrification when the Mersey Railway directors gave the go-ahead to Westinghouse for the big task that was to make the railway notable in one major respect, for it became Britain's first steam operated line to be converted to electric traction.

The arrival of Westinghouse on the Mersey Railway scene was none too soon — even while electrification was in progress the finances got worse and in 1902 the company did not even cover their working expenses, losing a total of £4,086. The passenger total for that bleak year was only 6,650,000. Nevertheless, better times were ahead and the company's troubles were nearly at an end.

Electrification of the line had to be carried out in the conditions imposed by steam working and involved, among other tasks, complete renewal of the track and equipping it for operation at 650 volts Direct current on the "fourth-rail" system with outside live rail and centre negative return rail. Refurbishing the stations and cleaning the tunnels was another big (and dirty) task, as it was found that soot lay two inches deep in places! Meanwhile the train services continued without interruption and by the end of April, 1903, the task was completed. The cost amounted to £300,000. The days of the powerful steam locomotives in the tunnels was now drawing to a close and a revolution in local rail transport was at hand. The Mersey Railway company looked forward to a future of increasing prosperity, which was inspired by the immense optimism of George Westinghouse, who viewed the conversion and its potential results with characteristic American confidence.

Before leaving the subject of steam traction on the Mersey Railway there remains a remarkable venture to recall. Between 1898 and 1900 a through-train was operated between Liverpool Central, Low Level station, and Folkstone Harbour, providing a connection for Paris! The outward train departed from Liverpool at 8.00 a.m., in the morning rush period, and it is to be hoped that no local passengers boarded it by mistake! The opposite working was an overnight train which arrived in Liverpool extremely early, at 6.30 a.m. These trains, which consisted of two or three Great Western Railway carriages were hauled by a Mersey locomotive to and from Rock Ferry. In addition, there was a train in each direction daily between Central Low Level and North Wales, the outward train ran to Corwen, whilst that in the opposite direction came from Ruabon. The service operated from 1898 until 1900. In 1898 a Liverpool—London, Paddington service was commenced, leaving Central at 7.57 a.m., arriving in London at 2.05 p.m. The opposite working departed from London at 12.10 a.m. This service lasted only a few months. These operations, sandwiched in between frequent local trains, must have provided difficulties. It is recorded that excursion trains from various far places were run through to Central Low Level in steam days.

In December, 1905 the Mersey Railway Company commenced to operate a motor-bus service between Birkenhead Central Station and Oxton, but had to discontinue it in March, 1906 due to an injunction. In May 1907 they began another motor-bus service, this time between Rock Ferry station and Port Sunlight, but this too, only lasted a short time, being discontinued in the following July. The last named route was of course, in direct competition with the trains on the L & NW and GW Joint Birkenhead—Chester line, a strange state of affairs, as the Mersey Company gained a great deal of patronage from passengers joining or leaving main line trains at Rock Ferry.

The Mersey Railway worked from early dawn until after midnight so that the last steam train and first electric train ran within a few hours of each other. Around midnight on Saturday 2nd May, 1903 a crowd assembled at Liverpool Central Low Level station to witness the end of an era. No doubt there were some who were sorry to see the end of steam, even if its going was a blessing in the particular circumstances. The final steam train was standing at the departure platform, whilst a band played a selection of popular airs. Scheduled departure time was 12.15 a.m. (Sunday morning) but with the lengthy ceremonial proceedings the train did not get away until 12.26 a.m. As the "Right Away" was given, the band broke into the strains of "Auld Lang Syne", but had to compete with what became a traditional ritual for last train ceremonies, a fusilade of explosions as the train passed over numerous fog signal detonators as it drew away, and as the tail lamp disappeared into the tunnel the men of the new electrical age were preparing for their complete takeover. After the train had gone silence descended on the station that would never again resound to the sounds of steam passenger trains. At each station detonators were exploded as the last train progressed on its journey to Birkenhead Park, thence to Bidston sidings of the Great Central Railway which had become a temporary resting place for Mersey Railway locomotives and rolling stock displaced by the new electric trains, which were assembled ready to take over the service.

Although training and trial trips had been run before the end of the steam era, few people had seen the electric trains. The current was off when the last steam train departed but was switched on in the early hours of the morning in preparation for the first day of electric traction. A train arrived at Liverpool Central to commence the service which was to be the normal weekday one envisaged under electric operation, and all trains were run empty until after the noon hour as a trial and rehearsal. In steam days the service commenced at 1.00 p.m. on Sundays but commencing on Sunday 11th October, 1903 the service was revised to commence at 9.00 a.m.

The weekday service allowed for a train every three minutes between Liverpool Central and Hamilton Square, alternate trains running to Rock Ferry and Birkenhead Park. Station stops were limited to 20 seconds durection but this was found difficult to adhere to initially, mainly through the unfamiliarity of the public with the exit and entry arrangements of the new trains and failure to quickly adjust to the tempo of the electric service. The first day's operation was carried through without a hitch, but on the Monday a cable fault at Birkenhead Park stopped the trains between 11 and 11.30 p.m. (they had late-night trains in those now far-off days!)

A party of press representatives was conducted over the railway on the first day of electric operation by James Falconer, Chairman of the company, R. Bowman Smith, Traffic Manager and Joshua Shaw, Electrical Engineer. They rode trains, visited the power station and finally retired to the Adelphi Hotel, Liverpool where they met the Lord

Mayor of Liverpool, the Mayor of Birkenhead and representatives of the British Westinghouse Electric & Manufacturing Company. All were impressed with the transformation in cross-river rail travel and admired the high, wide and handsome new trains with their Transatlantic looks and general air of efficiency.

Drivers of the steam locomotives were trained to drive the new electric trains during the night after the ordinary services had ceased (imagine such a procedure today!) They found a vast change in working conditions and now, instead of being exposed to smoke and steam, and adverse weather on the open-air sections, they sat in comfort behind plate glass and could read the signals clearly and see far ahead. The tunnel walls were no longer to be lit up by the glare from open fireboxes as locomotives were stoked but by vivid flashes from collector shoes and live rails of the new power medium which people were only just beginning to trust. Electricity was not in general use in those now distant days and people were not familiar with its mysteries as yet, though they appreciated the amenities which it made possible. Some people were actually terrified!

Upon electrification the company advertised seven features of the new services, as follows:

1. Complete abolition of smoke and steam.
2. Perfect ventilation by means of separate tunnels and electric fans.
3. Continuity of train service at short intervals rendering time-tables unnecessary.
4. Acceleration of trains.
5. Acceleration of lifts*, with improved entry and exit.
6. Comfort of passengers in commodious carriages.
7. Brightly-lighted carriages and stations.

* Electric motors replaced the steam pumping plant for lift operation.

The above just about summed up the advantages of the new era and the once unpopular railway now attracted large numbers of passengers so that it was not long before the Birkenhead ferries felt the effects of this formidable rival, which was destined to deplete their passenger loadings considerably.

The electrification project involved very much more than equipping the track. There was no power grid system available in 1903 so that it was necessary to build a generating station for traction and lighting current, and the site chosen for this establishment was Shore Road, Birkenhead, adjacent to the pumping station. The completed power house contained nine Stirling water-tube boilers, each with a working pressure of 170 lbs per square inch. Roney mechanical stokers carried fuel to the furnaces, and after depositing coal onto the grates, carried away the ashes, dumping them into wagons standing on a siding that curved sharply into the station from the dock railway on Shore Road. The three massive steam beam engines for pumping the tunnel were retained, but were replaced by electrical plant during the 1920's. One Hawthorne Davey engine was scrapped but the two other (Barclay) engines were retained on a standby basis until 1959. Now ancient machinery, beam engines in particular, seem to inspire pride and affection — even reverence in their attendants, and were often housed in buildings of an "ecclesiastical" character to impart the appropriate air of solemnity! The Mersey Railway beam engines were no exception to this rightful practice and until the last they were lovingly cared for and reposed amid scrubbed, polished and spotless surroundings. They were tall and could not be taken-in at a glance, towering into the twilight of the upper storey of the lofty building that housed them. Visitors were usually over-awed in the presence of such ponderous Victorian machinery and tended to speak in whispers as though they were inside a cathedral!

Although the steam pumping machinery was replaced by electrical plant during the 1920's, the old engines at Georges Dock, Liverpool were retained for emergency use, being in situ until after the close of World War II. Today four electrical pumps do the work, two at Liverpool and two at Shore Road, Birkenhead. A proportion of the water pumped out at Birkenhead is used to supply the municipal swimming baths. The four electrical pumps are completely adequate for the requirements of the railway today and though they lack the fascination of their predecessors, they occupy much less space! One Birkenhead engine is preserved.

On the electrical side the power station contained three Westinghouse generating sets, each of 1,650 horse-power, providing traction current at 650 volts, DC. There were also two smaller 300 horse-power sets to generate current for lighting and for the hydraulic lift pumps, the steam pumps being discontinued when the railway was converted. A huge bank of accumulators, filling an entire room, was installed as a safeguard in case of a major power failure, and these were capable of supplying sufficient current to bring every train safely out of the tunnels in the event of an emergency.

To the passer-by the most notable feature of the Mersey Railway power station was its tremendous round brick chimney towering to an altitude of 250 feet and which was a prominent landmark on Merseyside for more than half a century. It does not exist today, and neither does the power station, but this belongs to a later stage in the story.

A Mersey Railway steam train at Birkenhead Park station circa 1902. The "third" and "fourth" rails for electric traction are in position. The engine is No.8 "Birkenhead", which later went to Shipley Collieries.

Another view of a Mersey Railway steam train at Birkenhead Park immediately prior to the introduction of electric trains. Rain and steam lend atmosphere to the picture.

The Steam Engines Leave The Scene

Electrification of the Mersey Railway naturally rendered almost the entire stock of locomotives and carriages redundant and they were offered for sale by auction at the Great Central sidings, Bidston, this being held at 12.0 noon on Friday 26th June, 1903. The auctioneer was Geo. N. Dixon of Hanover Street, Liverpool, and he stated in his catalogue that prospective buyers of the locomotives would be able to see them in steam. The auction was not a success however. As a matter of fact the engines and carriages went away from Bidston in small numbers at a time, the last not departing until 1906, except for one locomotive which was retained for a time and did not leave the railway until 1908, of which more later.

The steam locomotives went to diverse destinations. Ten were bought by the Alexandra (Newport & South Wales) Docks & Railway Company, these being "Earl of Chester", "Duke of Lancaster", "Fox", "Mersey", "Victoria", "Bouverie", "Brunlees", "Tranmere", "Salisbury" and "Burcot". Four went very far from home — 11,000 miles in fact, to Australia, having been purchased by J. & A. Brown, Colliery owners in New South Wales. The engines concerned were "The Major", "Gladstone", "Liverpool" and "Connaught". To Shipley Collieries, Ilkeston went "Cecil Raikes" and "Birkenhead", whilst "Burnley" and "Banstead" migrated to Whitwood Colliery, Castleford, Yorkshire. The open-air footplates of all these engines were provided with shelter after they left Mersey Railway service. Those which were sold to the Alexandra Docks Railway passed into ownership of the Great Western at the Grouping and some of them were extensively "Great Westernised" eventually, and thus difficult to recognise as ex-Mersey Railway engines.

The old Mersey Railway locomotives disappeared slowly. Those which landed in the Great Western fold were withdrawn and broken up during the 1920's and early 1930's. The last one at work in Australia was "Liverpool" (ex-Mersey No.7), which was at Kalingo Colliery until 1943 and spent the last few years of its life stored out of use on a siding, exposed to the rigours of the Antipodean climate. Amazingly, No.1 "The Major", has survived, although withdrawn in 1930. It is to be restored as a museum-piece, but far from its original home.

Almost miraculously one Mersey steam locomotive remains here — "Cecil Raikes" (ex-Mersey No.5), which was employed for most of its active life on the mundane task of hauling coal trains between Shipley and Coppice Collieries in Yorkshire. This venerable old-timer was replaced by a diesel locomotive in 1956 and retired. Before finishing service "Cecil Raikes" worked just one more "passenger train", consisting not of coaches but open goods wagons in which rode a large number of railway fans, who by and large don't mind travelling in such a strange fashion! The trip took place at Shipley on Saturday 15th August, 1954, the train having been chartered by the Railway Correspondence & Travel Society.

The National Coal Board, last owners of "Cecil Raikes" recognised the historical value of the locomotive and donated it for preservation as a museum piece. At the time the British Transport Commission was in course of preparing a museum of transport in which locomotives and rolling stock of special historical or technical interest would find a place, and "Cecil Raikes" was hauled to Derby works of British Railways to await restoration and a place in the museum. Nothing was done to the engine however, and it still languished at Derby in 1965. About that time it became known that the Liverpool Corporation planned to add a Transport Gallery to the city museum, and what better candidate for inclusion than the old Mersey Railway locomotive?

British Railways subsequently presented "Cecil Raikes" to the Corporation of Liverpool and during February, 1965 the engine was greased-up and hauled Northwards for temporary storage on the Trading Estate at Kirkby, pending building of an extension to the city museum. After so long a period of standing still in complete idleness, the old engine felt the strain of the journey and sustained trouble due to bearings running hot. B.R. fitters were called to put things right and at length the engine arrived at Kirkby and was placed safely in a shed, to languish until March, 1967, when an undignified journey by road transporter was made to the City Engineer's depot at Breckside Park for overhaul and restoration to its original state. Unfortunately the old engine did not reach the city museum, for there was no room for it in the Transport Gallery, so it remained at Breckside Park for restoration work to be carried out. Little work was done on it however, and in August, 1978 the engine was removed to the Steamport Transport Museum at Southport (by road) and one hopes that "Cecil Raikes" will be restored in time for the Centenary of the Mersey Railway which falls in March, 1986.

As a final note of interest, it seems incredible that "Cecil Raikes" retained the brass condensing pipes all through its colliery service, even though they had not functioned since the engine had worked passenger trains on the Mersey Railway! The story goes that many years ago the pipes were removed, but the engineer in charge of the locomotives — who certainly had a soul and an appreciation for the fitness of things, ordered them to be restored lest the character of the engine be partly destroyed! It is an odd fact that although the Mersey Railway steam locomotives were built for hauling passenger trains, they all ended up on coal traffic, a job for which they proved to be eminently suitable, and were much more appreciated on this work than they were when working through the tunnels between Liverpool and Birkenhead!

Electrification did not see the complete end of steam on the Mersey Railway. Engine No.4 "Gladstone" was retained for use on permanent-way and engineer's trains, but being too big and heavy for this work, followed its colleagues to Australia in 1908. To replace it, a 4-4-0 Tank locomotive was obtained from the Metropolitan Railway of London in 1904. This was Metropolitan No.61, built by Beyer, Peacock & Company in 1884, and later rebuilt at Neasden, in 1908. This engine served the

Mersey Railway until 1925 when it was retired, worn out. Another 4-4-0 Tank, also ex-Metropolitan Railway, was then obtained. This was Metropolitan No.7 "Orion", built by Beyer, Peacock & Company in 1864, rebuilt at Edgeware Road subsequently, and twice again rebuilt — at Neasden in 1898 and 1921. The engine retained its characteristic and graceful form through all these rebuildings, and looked much as she always did except for the addition of a cab to shelter the crew. This splendid old locomotive lasted on the Mersey Railway as No.2 until 1939, being broken up at Birkenhead Park sidings during September of that year. Its Mersey livery was indian-red, lined out in black and gold.

To replace the old Metropolitan engine, an 0-6-0 Side Tank of Great Eastern Railway origin was obtained from the London & North Eastern company. This was L & NER No.7297 of Class J.66, which became Mersey Railway No.3 and was used on permanent-way duties throughout the 1939-45 war and beyond, surviving to be taken into the stock of British Railways on 1st January, 1948. The locomotive was sent to its home works at Stratford, London for a general overhaul in 1951, but was found to be beyond repair and condemned. Another former Great Eastern 0-6-0 Tank, number 68583 (ex-L & NER No.7256 of class J.67) was therefore allocated to the Mersey line, and this duly appeared under the arches on the Up side of the line at Birkenhead Central, where its predecessors were kept while not at work. About 1956 the engine was transferred to Mollington Street, former LMS and GWR locomotive depot, Birkenhead, but was transferred to Bidston, ex-London & North Eastern shed in 1957. In June 1958 this locomotive was scrapped at Gorton works, Manchester, and was not replaced. When a permanent-way or materials train required to work over the Mersey lines after that date a diesel-mechanical 0-6-0 shunting locomotive was used, one being borrowed from the small fleet of these machines that normally operated on Birkenhead docks. It will be seen then, that steam locomotives did not entirely disappear from the Mersey Railway until about 50 years after it was electrified!

In March 1968 what is believed to have been the first occasion of a main-line locomotive passing through the Mersey Railway tunnel took place, when a Class 47 machine worked through to Liverpool Central Low Level station (during the night) on clearance tests, with a view to using locomotives of this class on engineering trains in connection with new developments being considered at that time.

Wooden seats and pannelling in a Mersey Railway Third Class car as originally built. Note the sliding doors to separate smoking and non-smoking sections. (Photo: Mersey Railway Company.)

The more luxurious interior of a Mersey car in its later life. This is car No.95, photographed in September, 1953. (Photo: J.W. Gahan.)

Third Class Trailer car No. 29163 at New Brighton in September, 1953. (Photo: J.W. Gahan.)

Third Class motor unit No.34, still in red livery at New Brighton in September, 1953. it became BR 28427 and aquired green livery in November of the same year. (Photo: J.W. Gahan.)

A train of Mersey Railway clerestory cars in the stabling siding at Birkenhead Park in B.R. days. (Photo: G. Rose.)

A train of miscellaneous Mersey Railway cars laid up at Birkenhead North in August, 1956. The leading car is M28418. All were consigned to Horwich, for scrap. (Photo: J.B. Horne.)

From Carriages to Cars

Upon cessation of their service on the Mersey Railway the old steam-service carriages went to a variety of destinations far and near. Some were bought by the Liskeard & Looe Railway in Cornwall and went to work amid sylvan surroundings that were the very antithesis to the murky Mersey tunnels. Others went to railways in Wales — the somewhat mountainous Brecon & Merthyr, the industrial Rhondda & Swansea Bay, and rural Manchester & Milford (the latter which started life with great ambitions but got nowhere near its proposed terminals). The Garstang & Knott-End Railway in Lancashire bought a few, whilst some went to the neighbouring Wirral Railway. Some colliery companies obtained Mersey carriages for the purpose of transporting the miners to and from work.

One or two of the old carriages were retained by the Mersey Company for Departmental use. The Ballast Brake Van, No.1 which was a familiar object at Birkenhead Central until about 1956 was built on a former carriage underframe, whilst another carriage much in its original form survived for use on engineering trains until well into the days of British Railways. This latter vehicle, Mersey Railway No.2 retained its red livery and, with plates bearing the initials MTR (Mersey Tunnel Railway) was an object of great reverence among students of Mersey Railway history. Unfortunately both vehicles were scrapped before the preservation movement was started — they would be priceless treasures today!

The Mersey Railway electric rolling stock of 1903 consisted of 24 motor and 33 trailer cars — magnificent vehicles similar in design and construction to American railroad cars of the period, being large and roomy and featuring open platforms except at the driving end of each motor unit, which was totally enclosed, and, as can be imagined, these vehicles contrasted sharply with the four-wheeled arks which they replaced. The cars were each 60 feet long and were of American design in almost every detail, with clerestory roofs, small square windows, matchboard sides and massive truss rods. Buhoup combined buffer and centre couplings were employed, there being no side buffers. The four-wheeled trucks of the equalising beam type were fitted with small spoked wheels only 33 inches in diamater, and had a wheelbase of 6 feet. They were of Baldwin-Westinghouse design and were manufactured by the Baldwin Locomotive Works, Philadelphia. The car bodies were built by G.F. Milnes of Hadley, Shropshire, but four additional trailer cars of the same design were built in Birkenhead by G.C. Milnes Voss & Company during 1908, the trucks for the latter, also of existing design being maae by Mountain & Gibson of Burnley. The electrical equipment for the trains was supplied by the British Westinghouse Electric & Manufacturing Company of Trafford Park to whose works the completed motor units were taken to be fitted with their motors, control equipment etc.

The Third Class cars had longitudinal bentwood seats and interior woodwork of white ash. The seats in the First Class cars were mainly longitudinal with a few transversely situated, and were made of varnished cane. The interior panelling was in mahogany. Some of the cars were composite, with both First and Third Class sections but this arrangement did not last very long, separate cars for both classes being ultimately preferred. Second Class was not perpetuated on the electric trains, having vanished with the end of steam traction. The interiors of the cars were divided by sliding doors in order that smoking and non-smoking passengers could be separated, but these doors were removed in later years.

The livery of the Mersey electric trains was strikingly colourful — dark red with elaborate gold lining. The title MERSEY RAILWAY appeared on the fascia of each car just below the roof-line, whilst on the sides appeared the fleet number and crest of the company comprising the Liver Bird encircled by the full title — MERSEY RAILWAY COMPANY. This magnificent livery, somewhat simplified in later years lasted well beyond the date when the company was merged into British Railways and in fact, did not finally disappear until 1954. This was due to the fact that the vehicles were repainted at fixed intervals, being re-varnished in-between times so that it was several years before the whole fleet was dealt with and B.R. colours applied.

Entry and exit was originally through lattice gates on the end platforms, these being opened and closed by conductors, or "gatemen" as they were sometimes termed. Entrance to the saloon was by large sliding doors as in tramway practice. The employment of many men to operate the gates was uneconomical so commencing about 1912 the ends of the cars were enclosed. Partial enclosure was actually started earlier (in 1904) because it was found necessary to fit trailer cars with controls to facilitate splitting of trains in slack periods and using a trailer for driving from instead of having a motor unit either end. Fitting trailer cars with controls put the Mersey Railway among the earliest users of the multiple-unit system to universal today. Total enclosure meant that the typical American upright brake wheel had to be replaced by a wheel mounted in a vertical position on the bulkhead inside the vestibule. The enclosure also necessitated the fitting of large barn-like doors which opened inwards, and these were made in two portions so that if a trailer car was being used for driving the motorman could open the top half in order to lean out and observe signals during shunting etc. These large doors were not remotely controlled as in present-day practice, but were under the control of passengers, and it became a common practice, especially during the morning and evening rush hours for a certain element among the clientele to open the doors and leap out before the train had rolled to a stop, hordes of these "parachutists" racing up the short flights of steps to the lifts in an endeavour to get up street level before the main body. Travel in the rush hours was an experience indeed, with the cars packed almost solid with passengers.

The motor units were totally enclosed at the front end and from the beginning had the opposite end platform partially enclosed. Behind the driving compartment was a baggage section, with either side, a large sliding door, the exact counterpart of that on American baggage and express cars familiar in so many "Western" films and which conjured up visions of armed train robberies and bullion being unloaded out on the prairie or in the hills! There was little likelihood of such adventures on the Mersey Railway, however!

The motormen drove the trains by means of a small controller with a vertical handle shaped like the regulator handle of an early steam locomotive — the drum type main controllers were located at the rear of the compartment. These latter controllers regulated the supply of current to the motors, of which there were four per car, by electro-pneumatic apparatus, the motorman setting the process in operation by manipulation of the small handle in front of him. The operation of the pneumatic gear was accompanied by a great deal of "spitting" and "popping" whilst a miniature electric storm of blue lightning raged in the front and rear control compartments while a train was running. These compartments were lined with asbestos slate, and so were parts of the underframes in the vicinity of equipment likely to heat or flash. Air-blast sanding gear was fitted and this was occasionally called into use, especially on the steep climb between Green Lane and Rock Ferry where trains had to face the gradient from a standing start. This sanding gear was removed subsequently, a supply of sand being carried in bags thereafter, the motorman having to descend and sand the rails by hand when necessary, but this did not occur often.

The Mersey Railway trains were noted for their smooth and steady riding and comparative quietness, though at times some snatching of the couplings took place as a train was starting from rest. Even after 50 years of service the only real complaint that could be levelled against the trains was that the windows rattled — a fault that could easily have been cured. Motor hum and ringing of gears, often quite loud characterised the trains in their last years, however. Some Mersey men were of the opinion that the matchboard form of construction gave the cars a certain amount of resilience and enabled them to accommodate themselves to track undulations, but in latter days the matchboarding was merely simulated when repairs were carried out. The quiet running characteristics were possibly due to the remoteness of the wheels from the car floors, and the wheels being spoked instead of the more noise-producing disc type.

Additions were made to the fleet in 1923, 1925 and 1936, in which years a number of new cars were built, these featuring domed instead of clerestory roofs. The 1923/5 cars were constructed by Cravens of Sheffield and had timber bodies and matchboard pattern sides and ends. Those of 1936 were of composite construction — timber and lightweight metal panelling, and were built by the Gloucester Railway Carriage & Wagon Company. These additional cars were not formed into sets but were mixed with the earlier vehicles. Both the Cravens and Gloucester cars had metal treadplates on their steps into which the builders name was cast. This practice was followed by the LM & S Railway company, who carried out repairs to a number of Mersey Railway cars which had been damaged in wartime air raids, of which more later. A variety of bogie lengths and wheel sizes were introduced with these newer vehicles, whilst some had disc wheels instead of the spoked pattern.

An interesting and somewhat astounding feature of the Mersey Railway trains was that, although they had air brakes and air-operated control gear, they were not fitted with compressors, air reservoirs only being fitted to the vehicles. At the terminal stations the driver and guard each removed a metal cover from a grid on the platform and coupled a flexible hose into a compressed air main which gave a charge of air from an underground air compressor, this being sufficient to last through the next journey! This strange, expensive and time-consuming system lasted until 1938 when the Mersey trains underwent some changes which will be mentioned later.

Passengers looked with curiosity at the controller, air-brake gauge and handbrake wheel on each car platform. When trains were crowded at summer week-ends parents found the controller top to be a suitable seat for small children, whilst small boys would play at driving by holding the large brake wheel. Young faces stared or grimaced at each other through the large end windows at such times and much fun was enjoyed as the trains rolled steadily along with their characteristic wheel beat which went something like de-dum — de-dum. When viewed from an overbridge (in later years of course, when the sphere of operation had been extended) it was quite a fascinating experience to look down and see, beneath the car floor, the revolving axles and some interior bogie fittings, as there was quite an airy gap between the car body and wheels. This was not the case with the newer vehicles however which had British style bogies and larger wheels.

Although the Mersey Railway system was double track throughout, single line "staffs" such as this were used during engineering work when one track was closed for repairs. (Illustration: A. Astbury.)

A 1903 photograph of one of the new electric trains near Birkenhead Park. (Photo: Mersey Railway Company.)

The inclined pedestrian subway between Water Street and James Street stations, Liverpool. This passes beneath India Building and the Corn Exchange. It was threatened with closure in 1982, but has been reprieved. Photographed in October, 1982. (Photo: G. Jones.)

The dignified portal of the Mersey Railway company's Head Office at Birkenhead Central station. Photographed in 1982 after closure. Each door once carried a window with an engraving of the Liver Bird crest. (Photo: G. Jones.)

Mersey Railway cars under repair in the workshops at Birkenhead Central in 1953. (Photo: J.W. Gahan.)

The Years of Triumph

The Mersey Railway continued its independent existence through the Grouping of 1923, being one of the few railways to escape being drawn into the net of amalgamation. Traffic continued to increase and its financial position grew stronger as the years passed, the trials and worries of the first two decades long behind it.

Among the personalities on the Mersey Railway were its Chairman John Waddell J.P. His Grandfather, John Waddell, of John Waddell & Son, contractors, drove the experimental tunnel under the river back in the 1870's. His son, George became head of the business upon the death of John, and joined the Board of the Mersey Railway in 1893 and remained so until he died in 1919. The last John Waddell was **his** son, so the family name was associated with the railway for almost its entire history.

Two other famous Mersey Railway personalities were its General Managers, Joshua Shaw and Robert Varley. The former ruled the line soundly and efficiently from the year 1908 until 1935, whilst his successor, the company's engineer Robert Varley (who became General Manager and Engineer) was still in office when the line was Nationalised in 1948, and continued to operate it with great reliability for the general public. Another Biblical name was that of its power station chief — Mr. Abraham Pearson who joined the railway in 1914 and was still in charge when the station was closed in 1959.

The Mersey Railway worked in conjunction with the London Midland & Scottish (formerly Wirral Railway) at Birkenhead Park station through a Joint Committee, each company appointing a Chairman in alternate years. The boundary between the two systems was exactly midway along the platforms at Park Station, but this was overrun by both, for live rails penetrated into the LMS end so that shunting and stabling of Mersey trains could be carried out, whilst LMS steam locomotives entered Mersey territory in order to run round their trains. "Park" was certainly an interesting station in past days when steam locomotives took water, electric trains took air for their braking system and large numbers of passengers changed trains.

The London Midland & Scottish Railway had absorbed the Wirral Railway, the former partner in the joint station arrangement, at the Grouping of January, 1923. The Wirral company had considered electrification of their system as far back as 1900 but nothing further was done in that direction. In 1935 increasing traffic prompted the LMS company to revive the scheme, which was eventually put in hand. Commencing on Sunday 13th March, 1938 the Mersey Railway Company were given the operation of the Birkenhead Park—New Brighton line in exchange for Running Powers for the LMS between Park and Liverpool Central, thus abolishing the necessity for passengers to change trains on a journey from West Kirby or New Brighton to Liverpool and vice-versa. By that date most people had forgotten the through workings of Mersey Railway "steam" days.

In preparation for working over the Wirral lines, the Mersey Railway cars were thoroughly refurbished. The First class cars were provided with cushioned seats, in place of the previous rattan seating, whilst the Third Class vehicles received transverse leather seats arranged back-to-back. They were then set to work in company with the new electric trains of LMS design. As the Mersey trains were now required to work longer journeys, air compressors for the brakes and control gear were installed and the old system of charging-up from the underground mains was abolished.

Prior to 1938 no heaters were fitted to Mersey Railway trains, which might be considered to have been of no great consequence because no one was on a train for more than 15 minutes or so, and in this respect the trains were no worse than tramcars and buses which also had no heating. Whilst passengers waiting on a cold, bleak platform such as Rock Ferry, Birkenhead Central and Park would undoubtedly be glad to step into the shelter of a train, passengers changing from a snug steam heated train of the LMS/GW at Rock Ferry or from a cosy compartment on a Wirral train most certainly did not appreciate the "open plan" unheated Mersey Railway cars! Nevertheless, the Mersey trains did receive heaters eventually, in 1937-8 when they were refurbished for the longer journeys that they were required to undertake after the Wirral electrification was completed.

The Mersey Railway trains, after spending so many long years shuttling to and fro on their own short system found themselves travelling much further afield, out to New Brighton, passing docks, fields, golf links and sand hills where steam trains formerly operated (and continued to do so for goods and coal traffic). On Sundays they worked to West Kirby, the LMS trains then working the Liverpool—Rock Ferry service. In effect they exchanged workings, the object being to keep both Mersey and LMS men familiar with each other's routes and trains. On Bank holidays Mersey trains worked as extras to West Kirby as enormous numbers of passengers had to be handled at the terminus as well as at intermediate stations such as Moreton and Hoylake, which were in reach of popular beaches. Even though after a time one became used to seeing the Mersey trains at New Brighton, they somehow seemed to be out of place at West Kirby.

The live rail on the Park—West Kirby and New Brighton lines was placed in a position that differed from that of the Mersey Railway because new standards had been adopted for railway electrification equipment. This meant that the position of the Mersey live rail had to be altered. The work was carried out at nights after the last train had gone, and during the changeover period dual collector shoes had to be fitted to all Mersey trains to enable them to run on original and altered sections. These dual shoes were removed when the work was completed.

The old Mersey trains performed their countless journeys reliably year in and year out, and must have achieved a truly collosal mileage between them, mostly trouble-free. Repairs and overhauls were carried-out in rotation in the small works at Birkenhead Central, where near miracles were performed in an extremely cramped location. The long life and trouble-free service these old warriors rendered was sufficient testimony to the care and attention they received in this far-from-ideal group of small workshops.

During the air raids of 1940 and 1941 the Mersey Railway suffered a great deal of damage and although services on the 'open' sections were disrupted on several occasions the under-river section was never stopped despite serious damage to stations. Indeed, the Mersey system was an early victim for one night in September 1940, at the beginning of the severe attacks on Liverpool a bomb penetrated into Central Low Level station and exploded close-by two trains which were standing in the sidings beyond the passenger platform. Most of the cars forming these trains were badly damaged and one car was destroyed. Fast work on the part of the staff got the line cleared in time for the service to commence at its normal hour next morning!

Another incident which caused much damage to Mersey rolling stock was the explosion of a parachute mine just West of Birkenhead Park station. The fierce blast from this mine brought down part of the Duke Street bridge, damaged track and demolished the carriage shed. A Mersey train standing in a siding was badly shattered. Some of the bomb-damaged cars were sent to Wolverton works of the LMS company and extensively rebuilt.

So important was the Mersey Railway during the war period that the Wartime Railway Executive Committee arranged for the transfer of four six-car trains of London Transport rolling stock to Merseyside for use on the Mersey Railway in the event of any further losses by bombing. The trains concerned were composed of former Metropolitan District Railway (Hammersmith & City line) vehicles that had been made redundant by new trains but which had been reprieved from breaking up by the onset of the war, when to scrap rolling stock would have been most unwise. The four trains sent North were re-conditioned by London Transport and transferred to temporary LMS ownership. Two sets were stored at Birkenhead North and two at Hoylake, where they remained at rest due to the fact that no further emergency arose to threaten the Mersey Railway, it having survived the dreadful years of 1940-41 with no extra rolling stock — indeed they were minus on that score for a while due to the bomb damage. One interested observer noted the destination "Baker Street" on the indicator of one of the trains. It was a long way from the abode of Sherlock Holmes and was never to see its old metals again. Late in 1945 the London Transport trains were despatched to meet their delayed fate and were seen no more. They never turned a wheel in passenger service on the Mersey Railway or the LMS Wirral lines.

Upon Nationalisation of the railways on 1st January, 1948, the Mersey Railway exchanged its short and precise title for that of British Railways, London Midland Region, Mersey Section. There was little change at first and the trains continued to run in the red livery. Eventually car No.10 appeared with BRITISH RAILWAYS lettered in full on the fascia, in the position formerly occupied by the old title. Moreover, it still retained its Mersey red livery. Car No.34 was treated likewise. It was not until September, 1950 that the B.R. green paint was seen so far as ex-Mersey vehicles were concerned, when car No.53 (BR 28789) made its appearance in this rather miserable livery. Gone were the Mersey Liver Birds and lining, replaced by the new B.R. number in the centre of the fascia with the prefix M, and the Lion and Wheel emblem displayed on the side. Although all cars were renumbered, the old Mersey Railway number was painted on the end bulkheads for ready identification purposes — the maintenance staff knew every car individually and it would not have been an easy proposition to mentally equate the old and new numbers. Only one car managed to get its B.R. number on Mersey red livery, this being No.29184 (ex-Mersey No.103). The car numbers were transferred in gold-leaf on the interiors of the cars in Mersey Railway days but these were painted over after Nationalisation. The obliteration was not entirely successful however, because often enough the old number showed beneath the white paint.

Although the exterior of the Mersey Railway trains changed colour after Nationalisation, the interiors remained much the same as before except for the end platforms which received a rather billious shade of buff. The interiors of the baggage and motormen's compartments was green with buff ceiling, and buff clerestory in the case of the 1903 vehicles. As a matter of interest, the luggage section was indicated by the wording "Baggage Van" in earlier days — a strange juxtaposition of American and British terms!

Year after year passed by relentlessly without any hints of new trains, and by the 1950's it seemed as though the old Mersey trains would last for ever — indeed, some people hoped that they would! New rolling stock had replaced the 1904 trains on the Southport line in 1939, the Liverpool Overhead Railway company were rebuilding their old trains to modern standards, whilst the LMS Wirral train sets were only just over a dozen years old, but the Mersey trains continued their busy existence amassing more and more mileage. Newspaper editorials concerned about "old fashiondness" had long demanded their replacement, with little or no thought for their absolute suitability for the work which they did. However, well maintained as the Mersey trains were, age was beginning to tell and the cars were beginning to develop squeaks and rattles, also some slight body movement, but they were still considered by many regular travellers to be more pleasant to ride in than the much newer LMS trains which although having more comfortable seating and modern appointments are somewhat cramped for rapid-transit type service and give a bouncy ride plus a proneness to wheel "flats" and noisy running. One prominent newspaper feature writer, in a series of critical articles christened the Mersey line "Grandad's Railway" in view of various shortcomings real and imaginary, with particular reference to the old rolling stock, and as might have been expected this appelation appealed to Merseyside humour and soon appeared in chalk on station walls, and at least one train was embellished with the title "Grandad's Express"!

Intended to convey the utmost derision, the "Grandad" title could equally have been construed as a compliment, for Grandad's railways were usually well built and operated — the men of old not only aimed for reliability but usually got it, and slackness was not usually tolerated. The Mersey Railway was a case in point, for it was utterly reliable. Actually the newspaper campaign was mainly against the lack of paint and the dinginess of the stations, also overcrowding in the trains, but the latter could not be helped. The railway was built to carry crowds and performed its task admirably.

During the Summer of 1956, our newspaper writer was very pleased, for new train sets began to arrive and as each one was placed in service, a Mersey train was withdrawn. The first to go was not a regular set however, but a collection of six vehicles, only two of which were of the old clerestory design, the remainder being the newer domed roof cars. The cars concerned were M28418, 29174, 29181, 28799, 29182 and 28431. They were hauled away from Birkenhead North in the afternoon of Monday 27th August, 1957, the first of a melancholy procession over the next few months. With their smooth lines and in their shining new paint the replacement trains naturally made the "old faithfuls" look antidiluvian and rather woebegone, and their departure was the occasion of cheers and tears. Each Saturday a Mersey train, with seats and other fittings piled up inside, footsteps and collector-shoe gear removed, was shunted onto the little-used up-side loop at Birkenhead North Station, which began to acquire a polish after years of rust. A steam locomotive hauled each set away to Horwich for breaking up. It was like losing very old friends to see them depart, so familiar had the trains become over so many years, but the decree had gone forth that wooden rolling stock was outmoded, and repairs expensive, the vehicles life-expired, so they had to go.

Funnily enough, many people who decried the old trains regretted their demise soon afterwards. Each set was hauled away via the Wirral electric line to West Kirby, thence over the now closed single track from West Kirby to Hooton and from there onto the Ellesmere Port and

Helsby branch. The next stage of the journey was made via the main line to Warrington, then Wigan and so on to Horwich, the works of the former Lancashire & Yorkshire Railway, which, in addition to repairing steam and diesel locomotives, carried out overhauls to electric trains of the Southport, Wirral and Manchester—Bury lines. In passing, it is an interesting thought that when being hauled away for breaking up, the Mersey trains actually crossed over the river they had passed beneath countless times for half-a-century or so, but this time far inland, at Warrington.

One complete Mersey train remained in service for several months after all the others had been withdrawn, although a spare domed roof motor and clerestory trailer were kept at Birkenhead Central as standby vehicles, but no emergency arose to call them into service. The set train comprised cars Nos. M28427, 29186. 29189, 29193, 29187 and 28414, a mixture of clerestory and domed roof vehicles. The spares were Nos. M28428 Motor, and M29191 Trailer. Other cars also hung about for a time at Birkenhead Central including one earmarked for preservation (M28405, ex-Mersey No.1).

The last ex-Mersey train in service was eagerly sought-after by what the late Lucius Beebe called "the faithful" and B.R. revenue was increased a little through them keeping this old train in service because quite a few people rode on it specially, purely for its interest. At last, on Saturday 12th June, 1957 this venerable train was placed on the siding at Birkenhead North were it languished for a week, and on Monday 17th June ex-L&NWR "Super D" 0-8-0 No.49420 arrived from Birkenhead and hauled the train to Horwich for scrap. The remaining Mersey cars, Nos. M28411, 28421, 28428 and 29191 followed on 9th July and that was the end of the old rolling stock except for car No.28405 which went to a different destination, of which more later. The change in the character of the Mersey line was now complete. The replacement trains were generally similar to the LMS-designed Wirral sets.

Birkenhead Central station in 1982, still bearing the Mersey Railway title. The company's head office was situated at this station. (Photo: G. Jones.)

The Mersey Railway car shed at Birkenhead Central station. An extension has been added to accommodate longer trains. The former repair shops were at the rear of this shed – they were long and narrow, providing cramped working space. The former steam locomotive shed was situated in this area. Photographed in October, 1982. (Photo: G. Jones.)

James Street station, Liverpool in 1886. The building lasted in substantially the same condition until it was almost destroyed in the "Blitz" of 1941.

James Street station, Liverpool in 1982, the post-war replacement of the original station which was destroyed in the 'blitz' of May, 1941. (Photo: G. Jones.)

The Mersey line is not all tunnel! Trees and bushes at Birkenhead Park station, 1982. (Photo: G. Jones.)

A Mersey Railway train on the New Brighton service alongside a train of LMS stock at Birkenhead North. June, 1956. (Photo: J.B. Horne.)

Riding The Line in "Mersey" Days

Many memories of the Mersey Railway trains pass across the mind's screen when recalling them, and even today, on descending into the underground stations, one who was familiar with the old company still sub-consciously expects a "Mersey" train to arrive at the platform and would welcome the sound of a chime whistle once again in the cavernous depths. One remembers the crowds of passengers filing into the cars, or struggling to board at peak hours via the end platforms and the porters slamming the large barn-like doors (a duty they don't perform nowadays as all trains have remotely-controlled sliding doors). Then came the lurching start with the squeak of couplings and the steady glide away from the lighted platforms and into the blackness of the tunnel with blue flashes and little showers of "golden rain" playing about the collector shoes sliding on the live rail as the train receded.

It would be a wonderful experience to ride in a former Mersey Railway train again, and in order to bring back to mind what a journey on the line was like when the original electric trains were in their heyday an exercise in total recall and reference to past notes can provide some measure of satisfaction. A journey from Liverpool Central station to Rock Ferry can serve as an example. Such a journey is essentially the same today, of course, except for the type of train one travels on, but the old trains raised it from the ordinary to an experience of extreme interest if one felt the "mystique" of the subject. Perhaps it was the contrast between the transatlantic design of the Mersey trains — the unfamiliar, and the so familiar British aspect of almost all other rolling stock which gave a cross-Mersey journey its peculiar interest.

Imagine making a journey to Rock Ferry — in, for instance, the year 1939, when the Mersey Railway was still an independent concern and the unified nationwide system of British Railways was as yet undreamed of. Strolling along Ranelagh Street and entering Central Station via the main gates, those nearest to Lewis's department store which overlooks the arched glass roof of the Liverpool terminus of the Cheshire Lines Railway (there is another entrance further down the street and a subway to the Low Level station adjacent to the corner of Bold Street — at this time the most fashionable shopping thoroughfare in Liverpool) we proceed through the station concourse. Here we find a broad flight of stairs under a large sign which reads MERSEY RAILWAY — FREQUENT ELECTRIC TRAINS, and hurry past the large enamelled sheet-metal map which shows the system in relation to neighbouring railways. There is no need to consult the clock that overlooks the station concourse, for Mersey Railway train services are very frequent and trains run to Rock Ferry every few minutes. Central station's upper level resounds to the musical clanging of coupling rods, whistles and exhaust sounds of LNE and LMS locomotives that work to and from Manchester, Stockport, Southport and elsewhere on the Cheshire Lines system. Descending the stairway and mingling with many more potential passengers we pass into a subterranean world of quite different sights and sounds, and encounter that damp, musty tang of ozone and railway liquid soap familiar also on underground railways in London, Paris and elsewhere. The hum of electric traction motors falls faintly on the ears as we leave the domain of steam and stride along the lighted underground passageway with its bookstall, slot machines and advertising showcases, with the walls brightened by multi-coloured posters and railway timetables. People pass to and fro in the confined area, hurrying to and from the trains, for the Mersey is a very busy railway indeed, especially the Liverpool Central—Hamilton Square, Birkenhead section.

Arriving at the ticket office windows we tender our fares to the booking clerk, and after picking up the tickets that are ejected from a machine when the clerk presses a button, we descend a further broad flight of stairs and pass through the lattice gates onto the island platform, handing the tickets to the Examiner who clips them and passes them back. Above the platform is a large illuminated sign which lists the order of departures and we note from it that the next train but-one is for Rock Ferry. We do not need to look at the indicator to tell that the LMS train standing at the platform is not the one we want (unless it was Sunday) for these trains work exclusively on the West Kirby service on weekdays, but not all passengers know that however. The train is of smaller dimensions than those of the Mersey, and its red livery is enhanced by the crest of its owning company, bearing the English rose, Scottish thistle and Welsh leek implying far-flung activities in contrast to the Liver Bird of the purely local Mersey system.

Shortly before departure time for the LMS train, a faint rumbling in the tunnel heralds the approach of another, and as it draws near we can tell from the sound of its motors that it is a Mersey company's train — which it is, and the station suddenly becomes a hive of increased activity as this train draws majestically into the Up face of the island platform and comes to a halt with a long sigh as the air in the brake cylinders is exhausted. The large doors at each end of the cars are flung open and crowds of passengers stream out and make their way towards the platform exit.

A sudden rumbling of automatic doors closing and the shutting of the platform gates indicate the imminent departure of the LMS train which, upon the driver receiving the bell signal from the guard (and observing that the starting signal is green) draws away rapidly into the tunnel, its red tail lamp receding in the darkness and intermittent flashes from its collector shoes illuminating the tunnel walls. As soon as the train has gone, the platform gates are thrown open once again and more passengers surge through. The gates are closed just before the departure of a train so that last-minute passengers cannot dash through and try to board a train in motion — something they cannot do with the LMS trains however. People spread out along the length of the platform — some occupy the seats, others stand, some read newspapers whilst others gaze into the various showcases in which local firms display selections of their merchandise.

The driver and guard of the newly-arrived train exchange places, the guard boarding the East end of the train lately vacated by his colleague, who now occupies the West or Birkenhead end, which is still the rear, but will shortly become the leading end. After ascertaining that all is in order and that the signal is showing green, the guard raises his oil-lit hand lamp, signalling the driver who next "backs" the train into the long head-shunt in the tunnel beyond the platform and after it has cleared the electro-pneumatically operated points, they shift over with a sharp hiss, the signal changes and the train next draws forward into the Down side of the island platform. On coming to a stop the waiting passengers file in and settle themselves on the leather seats or First Class cushions. From the station loudspeaker a mysterious, recorded male voice announces "Hamilton Square, Birkenhead Central, Green Lane and Rock Ferry train". After a few minutes have elapsed, a whistle is blown by the platform inspector, porters slam the car doors and with a slight lurch and snatch of couplings the train commences to move and glides out of the station in that dignified "Mersey Railway" manner. Wheel flanges whine dully as they encounter the curved rails beyond the platform end and the train thuds its way through the trackwork of the two crossovers, whilst the car lights blink off and on again as gaps in the conductor rail are reached. The hum of the motors rises in pitch as speed is increased and the beat of the wheels on the rail joints quickens, only to slow-down again as power is shut off and the brakes applied for the stop at James Street station, the lights of which quickly dispel the darkness outside the train windows and present a vision of a crowded platform, whitewashed brickwork and posters. More people come aboard — those not able to find seats hang onto the standee straps, some holding on with one hand whilst gripping a folded newspaper in the other and endeavour to read as they ride. Men with brief cases, women with shopping bags and baskets, people laden with parcels, and small children all jostle for space in the crowded car.

The train is soon on the move again, accelerating in that steady "Mersey Railway" fashion for the three-minute run beneath the river. A woman says to her small son "there are boats above us now, up there" and he asks how so? The question brings forth some attempt at an explanation of how the railway passes under the river. Mersey maintenance men say that the sound of ships propellers penetrates the rock above the tunnel — they can actually hear it! Speed increases and the car's lights flicker as the collector shoes bounce on the live rail sending out blue flashes that reveal the brickwork of the tunnel like vivid night-time lightning, something that children, with noses pressed against the window panes, watch with awe or delight. On looking along the length of the car, one can see, through the large end windows the adjacent vehicle which seems to be performing a merry dance as it travels, bouncing and lurching, but little or no discomfort is felt by seated passengers whilst the standees accommodate themselves to the motion. The motors whine on full power as the train rushes headlong down the gradient to mid-river and then suddenly, the upward grade is felt through a slight lifting sensation and the speeding motors now begin to feel the 1 in 30 rise, the whining turns to a deep hum and next becomes a laboured groaning as the heavy train ascends towards Hamilton Square, into which station it enters, thudding over the crossover points, in just three minutes from James Street, and draws to a halt. A great many passengers leave the train here, the under-river section of the line being the most heavily used and passengers hurry up the stairs, over the footbridge and into the lifts to take them up to street level and the buses of Birkenhead Corporation and the Crosville Company. Over the way lies Woodside passenger station of the LMS/GWR Joint lines, and the docks of Grayson, Rollo & Clover, also Cammell-Laird, whilst just around the corner is stately Hamilton Square after which the station is named.

Once more car doors are slammed shut and the train is on its way, and after crossing the junction at which the line to Birkenhead Park diverges, runs directly beneath Hamilton Street and in a couple of minutes emerges into daylight at Birkenhead Central station, which is quite a large one, situated in a wide cutting. It features a platform and signal box on the West side, and an island platform on the East side, both platforms having elaborate glass awnings on iron columns. There are three footbridges at this station, one of them for use by staff only. Sidings and carriage sheds, workshops and sundry other buildings fill the rather narrow area between the station and the sandstone wall that borders the Birkenhead gas works, the large gasholders of which loom above the Mersey Railway premises. Spare trains stand in the sidings awaiting the evening rush hour when they will be called into service to help with the transport of many hundreds of passengers making their way home from work, after which they will retire again, leaving the regular trains to handle the evening town-goers. Cars awaiting works attention stand about, looking distinctly odd when not coupled to others, and there are usually a few goods wagons here, most of them being from the main line companies. These are normally hauled about the premises by an electric car instead of a locomotive.

After leaving Birkenhead Central, the train passes through a short length of cutting with grassy slopes on the Up side and the works buildings on the Down, and into tunnel again, passing on the right a series of arches parallel to the track behind which the company's solitary steam locomotive is kept when not in use. A few moment's run in the darkness brings the train to Green Lane station, which is situated in a cutting, with massive sandstone retaining walls either side, through which moisture continually seeps causing moss and weeds to grow liberally in the crevices. The station is a gloomy one with glass awnings and massive transverse steel strengthening girders spanning the rails. A huge enamelled sign reads "ALIGHT FOR TRANMERE AND CAMMELL-LAIRDS". The aspect of Green Lane station from the street is far superior to that from the platforms, for it is an imposing and well-designed red-brick building situated in a residential thoroughfare off the main road.

After leaving Green Lane station the train climbs the steep gradient of about 1 in 36 out of the tunnel and emerges onto an embankment beside the multi-track Chester—Birkenhead main line. From the train a splendid panoramic view opens up across the Mersey — the Cathedral-dominated buildings of Liverpool, the South Docks, with the tall shipyard cranes towering high in the foreground, whilst on either side of the railway there are narrow residential and industrial streets dating from the 19th century. On the right-hand side several sidings, which accommodate Mersey Railway ballast wagons run into a long building that was a carriage shed in the railway's steam era (it was destined to be destroyed in the wartime blitz and the sidings were later removed). As the train runs beside the main lines we are quite likely to see a train of red LMS coaches hauled by a green Great Western locomotive, or perhaps GWR chocolate-and-cream vehicles with a black LMS engine at the head on this jointly operated length of railway. It is not far now to Rock Ferry, the approach being heralded by the tall ex-L & NWR signal box, and the Mersey train draws into the large station, coming to a stand in the Mersey Railway bay platform, the main lines continuing right through. Here the ritual of changing places is repeated by the crew, and the train is ready for yet another journey in its busy life.

Certain Mersey trains provided connections with main line steam trains to and from Chester, and in the Northbound direction, both steam and electric trains sometimes pulled out of Rock Ferry station simultaneously, running neck-and-neck until the Mersey train dipped down into the cutting to plunge beneath the streets. Both the LMS and GWR 2-6-2 Tank engines employed on the Chester—Birkenhead trains had good powers of acceleration and passengers always enjoyed such "races" which enlivened what many people considered a rather dull journey because of the tunnels.

The reactions of strangers on encountering the extremely un-British style Mersey trains depended upon from whence they hailed. To the American visitor they were just like "rapid transit" trains in his own country as he surprisingly discovered. To the Londoner they resembled the older Metropolitan and District Railway trains but people from anywhere else in Britain had seen nothing like them. After riding on one of the smaller-dimensioned LMS Wirral trains the interior of the Mersey cars was like a cathedral compared to a parish church, so lofty and spacious did they seem to be, giving plenty of standing room as well as seats. Indeed, they were almost ideal for the work they performed. Through communication was provided between the cars, but was not for the use of passengers however. Lazy tongs stretched between cars to prevent people getting between or trainmen from falling out when passing from one car to another. The trains did not seem to burst into the stations like London Tube trains or their LMS Wirral counterparts, but emerged majestically from the tunnels and rolled to a steady and dignified halt.

Inside each car large enamelled metal notice plates in blue with white lettering bore the following requests: RIDE INSIDE THE CAR AND NOT ON THIS PLATFORM, also DO NOT ALIGHT UNTIL THE TRAIN HAS STOPPED. Both these instructions were ignored to some extent, especially during peak hours when the end platforms provided some welcome additional standing room.

The stations in the tunnel sections of the Mersey Railway are of typical underground railway character, lined with bricks and whitewashed. They are of enormous spaciousness, having been built for steam traction. Lighting was originally by gas, a four-inch main being laid through the tunnel, connected to the Liverpool Gas Company's main and to a gasholder of the Birkenhead Corporation Gas Department. Electric lighting was installed when the railway was electrified and today fluorescent tubes provide the modern touch. Electric lifts have long taken over from the old "flying ballrooms" the replacement of which began in 1936, and what these 60-passenger Wadsworth lifts lack in capacity compared with their predecessors is made up for in speed. Additional lifts have been provided at James Street and Hamilton Square in recent years to deal with the increasing passenger flow. There was no room for the installation of escalators at any Mersey Railway station and lifts were therefore the only alternative even if they possess some disadvantages. One each of the old hydraulic lifts were retained at James Street and Hamilton Square stations until about 1961, for use in peak periods and on Bank Holidays until sufficient lifts of the new type had been provided. The electric lifts run at a speed of 400 feet per minute with a load of 60 passengers equivalent to about four tons in weight. Originally the lifts had a loudspeaker warning — "Stand clear of the gates" but these are no longer operative.

James Street station was in the midst of an area that was heavily pounded by bombs and extensively damaged by fire during the 1939-45 war and did not escape severe damage. During the "May Blitz" of 1941 all the upper floors and the hydraulic lift tower were so badly damaged that they had to be demolished and as a consequence the premises were closed for several days while clearing up was in progress. All the lifts were out of action for seven months, so that passengers were obliged to use the long pedestrian subway to and from Water Street which penetrates as far down as the lower extremity of the lift shafts, a flight of steps giving final entry to the platforms, which are linked by a footbridge. This subway emerges at the North West corner of India Building, the huge commercial block in Water Street which replaced an older building in 1928. A similar subway leads from Hamilton Square station to Shore Road in Birkenhead but is used in peak periods only, unlike its Liverpool counterpart which is open all day, but is not now opened on Sundays.

Liverpool Central Low Level station had an extremely narrow island platform for many years, which eventually became totally inadequate for the passenger traffic it had to deal with. In 1927 a decision was made to widen this platform and the difficult task was carried out over one week-end without interruption to the intensive train service — a masterpiece of planning and execution. In this operation the former Up line had to be abandoned and the erstwhile engine siding of steam days became the Up main line. Further work was carried out at Central Low Level in 1936 when the tunnel was extended to accommodate six-car trains, made necessary by the ever-increasing traffic.

The names of the Mersey stations appeared on large diameter circular blue-enamelled plates placed every few yards on the station walls, and these survived well into the British Railways era. They were eventually replaced by smaller signs in B.R. red and white. These were not so easy to read as were their predecessors, even though station lighting was greatly improved.

A distant view of the power station chimney at Birkenhead, taken from Shore Road in 1961. Note the scaffolding on the chimney, about to be demolished. (Photo: J.B. Horne.)

Hamilton Square station, Birkenhead in 1886. Note the pinnacle at the top of the hydraulic tower, which was removed long ago. A horse-drawn tram is visible in Canning Street alongside the building.

The hydraulic tower at Hamilton Square station, Birkenhead, 1982. A similar tower at James Street, Liverpool was destroyed during the 'blitz' of May, 1941. (Photo: G. Jones.)

Green Lane station, Birkenhead in 1982. The bridges in the background carry the freight lines to Birkenhead docks (formerly LMS and GW Railways). (Photo: G. Jones.)

A general view of the partially modernised station at Rock Ferry, in 1982. A train for Liverpool awaits departure time whilst a diesel train for Chester stands at the former main-line platform. (Photo: G. Jones.)

The Signalling System — Past and Present

The original signalling on the Mersey Railway was a semaphore system installed by the Railway Signal Company of Fazakerley, Liverpool, the telegraph being by John Lavender, telegraphic engineer, of Manchester. Post office wires and those of the Telephone Company were laid through the tunnel, thus obviating the otherwise long detour via Runcorn. Each station had a signal box and, rather astoundingly, there was a box situated in mid-tunnel under the river, known as River Cabin, which, however, was manned only in the morning and evening peak periods to shorten the length of the block sections and allow a greater number of trains to be handled. The signalman in this lonely box must have inhaled plenty of sulphur from the steam locomotives passing every few minutes on their headlong dash towards Liverpool or Birkenhead. Not for him the fresh air and extensive views enjoyed by men in other lonely signal boxes in remote places, or even from those situated nearby on the Wirral lines. The men who worked in the tunnel signal box had to walk to and from their hole in the wall domain. There could be few railway signalmen who had to carry out their duties beneath the bed of a river! When the semaphore signalling was replaced, the River Cabin was closed.

Today the signals on the Mersey line are two-aspect colour lights, with automatic train stops, the signals themselves being Westinghouse automatic and semi-automatic types. This signalling, installed in 1921 and since modernised is operated by track circuits at all locations except Liverpool Central, Hamilton Square, Rock Ferry and Birkenhead Park. Signal boxes were provided at these places.

The working of the terminal at Liverpool Central, until the alterations in 1977 was normally automatic, on a system that was introduced in 1923. Trains, sorted at Hamilton Square, arrived at Central in the correct sequence. An arriving train halted at the island platform, and its subsequent movements were governed by timing relays. The double track continued beyond the platform into a dead-end tunnel, but the Down track only was used, the other line being employed as an over-run or trap siding, for which the points were normally set and would divert a train that overran the platform or moved off against a red signal. Twenty seconds after a train had stopped the relay moved the points and the signal cleared for the train to move ahead into the headshunt, and provided that the Down side of the platform was clear, the points automatically altered and the signal cleared to allow the train to reverse into the platform on the side opposite to that at which it had originally arrived. The track-circuiting ensures that a train sets the signal to red after it has passed and this signal will not clear until the train has passed a safe distance beyond and set further signals to red behind it.

With this system in use any train that should overrun a signal that was at danger would have its brakes automatically applied by the track-side trip mechanism. The system embraces Home, Starting Intermediate and Overlap signals and was designed to handle extremely heavy traffic with safety and efficiency. Two emergency signal boxes were provided at Liverpool Central, one, known as East Box being situated beyond the station platform. The other one, West Box was in a recess cut into the rock at the West end of the station in the tunnel. There was another emergency signal box at James Street, which could be switched in if the automatic system failed.

In the event of a mishap at Liverpool Central, automatic working could be cut out and the signal boxes brought into use and trains could reach either face of the island platform via facing and trailing crossovers that are situated in the tunnel at the station approach. Each intermediate station has a crossover in case a mishap necessitates short workings or a shuttle service to be operated. Such emergencies have occurred but seldom, so that the rails of the crossovers are usually dull and oil-covered in contrast to the brilliant polish of the intensively used running rails.

Beyond Birkenhead Park where the Mersey Railway trains operated after 13th March, 1938 the signalling was, and still is to some extent of the semaphore type, with upper quadrant arms, but colour lights are gradually replacing these. Beyond Green Lane on the Rock Ferry line semaphore signals worked by the station signal box are still employed, some vintage L & NWR specimens still being in use until well into the 1950's. A new signal box of brick construction was built to replace the former L & NWR box in 1956.

(486 O.) **Mersey Railway.** (A supply of these Forms must be kept in each Signal Box.)

[RULES 222 & 223 (b).] WRONG LINE ORDER FORM "C."

Authority for Engine Driver to travel on the Wrong Line in case of Accident.

To Driver of Engine No. ________ working ________ m. Train

From ________________ to ________________

I authorise you to return with your Train on the Wrong Line to this Signal Box.

Signature of ________________ Signalman

at ________________ Signal Box.

Date ________ 189__ **Time issued** ______.m.

Catch Points exist at ________________

[SEE OVER.

The Years of Change and Development

The seemingly changeless Mersey Railway carried on in its own way until 1938, when through working with the LMS commenced — the first major change since the dawn of the electric era. The original Mersey Railway fourth rail system lasted a long time — until 1955 in fact, when it was changed to third-rail to conform with the system adopted by the LMS company when they electrified the West Kirby and New Brighton lines, thus the old Mersey trains operated entirely on the third-rail system for the last few months of their long lives. As the latter trains ran over the Wirral lines after March, 1938 they had to be equipped with a change-over device whereby the earth-lead could be altered from centre rail to running rail. The LMS trains also had such a device to perform the opposite function to enable them to run on the Mersey lines. The change-over point was at Birkenhead Park station where a permanent-magnet was installed between each set of rails to automatically actuate the changeover switches. These were of course, done away with when the change to third-rail was completed.

The year 1959 saw the end of the old Mersey Railway generating station at Shore Road, Birkenhead. It was no longer economical for the railway to take current from its own source of supply, mainly because the original Westinghouse equipment was reaching life-expiry and, from 25th June, 1959 all supplies have been taken from the national grid. That date marked the end of an era and did not pass without official recognition, for the shut-down of the premises was marked by a small ceremony in which the principal participant was Mr. Robert Varley, last General Manager of the Mersey Railway, who actuated the switches that silenced the old generating plant for ever. Then began the dismantling of the once busy and vital premises, only a portion of which continued in use, for tunnel pumping purposes. The siding from Shore Road was removed, the generating plant reduced to scrap and finally the most notable feature of all, the 250-foot brick chimney was demolished, leaving a gap in the landmarks of Birkenhead. In September, 1961 the chimney was surrounded by scaffolding, then dismantled brick-by-brick, an operation that had to be carried out with great care due to its proximity to the busy main road leading to Woodside ferry and bus terminal. Today there is little left of the former nerve centre of the old Mersey Railway.

Although the Mersey Railway was intended to be primarily concerned with passengers, goods traffic was also envisaged to and from the Liverpool docks. In 1885 the company applied for Powers to construct a goods branch from a point West of James Street station, passing under Bath Street and surfacing at Dundee Street opposite Waterloo Dock, where connection was to be made with the lines of the Mersey Docks & Harbour Board. The Act was granted and a short length of tunnel was actually bored for the purpose, but the scheme was dropped. Goods traffic would have been almost impossible in the daylight hours and for most of the evenings also, as the intensive passenger service left no spare paths for additional trains, especially loose-coupled goods trains that would have been difficult to control on the gradients. Even the hours between midnight and dawn would have proved unsuitable as track and tunnel maintenance had to be carried out during the few hours when trains were not operating.

Although they had no goods traffic, the Mersey company possessed a number of low-sided open ballast wagons and flat wagons which they used on track maintenance and engineering work. These were painted light-grey and bore the initials M.E.R. A simple M.R. would possibly have led to confusion with the far-flung Midland Railway! These wagons were scrapped soon after Nationalisation and British Railways wagons used thereafter.

The Mersey section of the present-day British Railways system will no doubt be always referred to as the Mersey Railway by the people of Liverpool and Birkenhead. It will also, no doubt, continue to carry millions of passengers annually and provide the quickest mode of travel beneath the river. It is one of the busiest stretches of railway in Britain — indeed, the junction at Hamilton Square is, at peak traffic times, one of the most intensively used in the whole country with train following train at very brief intervals. The line is assured of a sound future as a result of recent developments and extensions.

Plans for developing the Mersey Railway were in existence for many years, but owing to lack of finance, nothing was done and it seemed as though the system would remain in its original form for evermore, but in the fullness of time action was commenced, resulting in the useful Loop Line now in operation. Construction of this facility came about mainly as the result of the formation of the Merseyside Passenger Transport Executive which, taking over various municipal bus services and the Mersey ferries, commenced to function on 1st April, 1969. Inter-working with British Railways in respect of local train services was in the brief of the MPTE, the function of which is to provide a properly integrated passenger transport system in the Merseyside area, on both sides of the River Mersey.

Studies of local transport needs were made from time to time by various bodies in the post World War 2 period, but no action was taken so far as railways were concerned until after the MPTE had come into existence. This body acted upon the results of the Merseyside Area Land Use/Transportation Study, published in July, 1969, recommending, among other things, the construction of the long envisaged Mersey Railway Loop, a scheme which would increase the capacity of the system by transforming the Liverpool Central Low-Level from a terminal to a through station, thus cutting out shunting and reversals. The scheme would also enable the railway to serve additional areas of the city of Liverpool together with its most important station — Lime Street, and result in enormously increased facilities for passengers. In March, 1970, the British Railways Board authorised the scheme and so, the talk of many years at last turned to positive action. In April, 1971 the Department of the Environment agreed to make a grant of 75% of the cost of construction, the MPTE providing the balance. The new works were designed to enable the frequency of the train service on the cross-river section of the railway to be increased from 24 per hour to a possible maximum of 40, and the carrying capacity from 15,600 passengers per hour to the enormous figure of 26,000.

The Terminal Loop as the new project was known, consists of a single track, entirely in tunnel, veering from the existing line at a point a little distance West of James Street station (using as its commencement the short length of tunnel which was excavated in the early days for the proposed goods line to the North Docks) and curving to pass below Moorfields, at which a large new station has been built. It next proceeds round to Lime Street passing below the main-line station which had a low-level platform provided, and then curves round to Central station, after which it proceeds in a Westerly direction, rejoining the original line near South Castle Street. Although both Exchange and Central main-line stations have been closed, the New Moorfields station has replaced the former in the commercial district of the city, whilst a new Mersey Line deep-level station at Central now serves the shopping centre. The former Mersey Railway station of Central Low-Level has been transferred to the associated Link Line which handles trains that formerly used Exchange station.

Under the new arrangements all trains travelling into Liverpool from Birkenhead proceed round the loop, stopping at a new platform at James Street, thence onward to serve Moorfields, Lime Street, and back to James Street, by this point on their way out of Liverpool. There are no reversing operations at Central Deep-Level as there were at the former Low-Level station, as trains do not run into a dead-end terminal as they did previously. Construction of the Loop has greatly increased the capacity of the Mersey line, as well as giving it the advantage of distributing passengers over a wider area of the city, also giving more convenient travelling facilities within the city centre.

On the Birkenhead side of the river, a burrowing junction has been constructed at Hamilton Square station which, in cutting out conflicting train movements at the junction where the Rock Ferry, West Kirby and New Brighton lines diverge, has enabled that station to handle the increased train service that the Loop Line made possible.

Construction of the Loop Line commenced in February 1971, with the sinking of working shafts on land between Moorfields and Vernon Street, in William Brown Street, Central Station and at Mann Island, the latter in the old Great Western Railway goods yard. In Birkenhead shafts for the burrowing junction were sunk in Canning Street and Lorn Street. Construction work was carried out for British Rail by the contractors Edmund Nuttall Ltd., the planning and design work being performed by British Rail architects and engineers. Consulting Engineers were Messrs. Mott, Hay & Anderson. Concrete and steel were used throughout the tunnel, with the rails laid on concrete which unfortunately tends to make the trains noisy, in contrast to the old Mersey Railway tunnel which is brick-lined, the rails being laid on timber sleepers in crushed stone ballast and is thus quite sound absorbing. The change in sound is apparent where a train passes from old to new tunnel or vice-versa.

After a little over two-and-a-half years work, the tunnel, which was bored in two separate sections was completed, the final breakthrough between the two sections being made at a point beneath Lime Street on Monday, 8th October, 1973, accompanied by appropriate ceremony. During construction thousands of tons of spoil needed to be disposed of, much of it being removed by rail, necessitating the provision of two motive power units which could run on their own batteries, or by power from the live rails on existing lines. Two such battery-electric locomotives were adapted from British Railways Southern Region design electric motor coaches from the Euston—Watford (London) suburban line, to haul trains of spoil away. They were given the numbers DM 975178 and DM 975179. These have been retained for use in the tunnels during track repairs or engineering work and are normally stabled at Birkenhead North.

The Loop Line was completed early in 1977 and was opened for passenger traffic on Monday, 9th May, with a revised and more intensive train service. Its usefulness was immediately apparent, though owing to work not having been fully completed at Moorfields and Lime Street stations, Loop Line trains did not call at these initially. The official opening at the Link and Loop Lines was performed at Moorfields station by Her Majesty The Queen on 25th October, 1978, after all the works had been completed.

It is an interesting thought that the Loop Line and its associated Link Line are the first new railways on Merseyside since the late Liverpool Overhead Railway was completed far back in the year 1893. It is all the more encouraging therefore that these new lines have been brought to completion during what might well be termed an anti-railway era in which many persons, including some in high transport circles considered that construction of new railway extensions was flying in the face of progress. Such thinking has largely been reversed however and Merseyside is well in step with many of the World's most important cities in developing rail transport to save energy, decrease pollution and solve traffic problems.

Signalling on the Loop Line is provided by multiple-aspect Colour-lights as in the already existing Mersey Railway tunnels. A new control centre has been brought into use at James Street station replacing all former Mersey Railway signal boxes in the tunnel sections. It also controls the Link Line as far out as Bootle Junction and Kirkdale on what were formerly main lines handling both goods and passenger traffic, though little of the former passes over these lines nowadays.

The routing of the Loop and Link Lines within the city of Liverpool has resulted in the abandonment, for passenger traffic, the section of former Mersey Railway tunnel between Paradise Street and a point East of James Street station. This section retains a single line of rails only and is used for transferring Southport and Ormskirk, also Garston line trains between their own section and the workshops at Birkenhead North, a much shorter journey than the one they had to make since the repair works at Meols Cop, Southport were closed down. The long haul round via Liverpool, Earlestown, Warrington and Chester was no longer necessary after this short cut became available. The section of ex-Mersey Railway tunnel between Paradise Street and Central station is now used by Link Line trains, the Mersey trains now of course having their own new tunnel which breaks into the original one East of James Street station. The Eastbound platform here is now out of use except in an emergency, whilst the platform, completely refurbished is used by westward-bound trains making their way round the Loop.
round the Loop.

An unwelcome problem, one that plagued the former Mersey Railway Company, now gives Merseyrail engineers a headache, namely the influx of water. Underground springs abound in the area near the river Mersey and water from some of these is entering the tunnels at an increasing rate. Much of this water was formerly used by industries within the city and thus a considerable amount of it was diverted away from the railway. The closure of many industrial plants in recent times has resulted in the sub-surface water table rising, and the penetration of the tunnels is now a problem, as the water can rise to a level at which it short-circuits the electrical signalling and thus disorganises train services. Additional pumping plant is having to be provided to get rid of this unwelcome intruder.

A considerable amount of water pumped from the old Mersey Railway tunnel is used to supply the Birkenhead Corporation swimming baths, whilst some from the new Loop Line tunnel is used in the Liverpool Echo building to remove excess heat.

The Loop Line has been a success right from the day it commenced operation, and is an immensely popular facility. In spite of recent troubles (the industrial recession and unemployment) passenger use at the Merseyrail network increased by 27% during the first three years of operation, the under-river section taking a fair share of this. Many passengers have ceased using buses and ferries to make use of the better facilities provided by the upgraded rail system, whilst large numbers of car owners now make use of the train for travel to and from business. The Loop has also made for easy and convenient interchange between the

Mersey/Wirral lines and those to Southport, Ormskirk, Garston, Kirkby, St. Helens, Manchester, Crewe, and the main-line trains at Lime Street.

With the many alterations of recent years, there is little to remind today's travellers that there was once such a body as the Mersey Railway Company, as only a few traces that signified the line's former ownership remained after the departure from the scene of the old Mersey rolling stock, but in one or two places the company's title could still be seen, for a time. A sign at the entrance to the Water Street subway in Liverpool proclaimed MERSEY RAILWAY until it was replaced by a British Rail sign in 1971, whilst a similar sign spanned the entrance to Liverpool Central Low-Level station until well into the 1960's. Indeed, in 1982 the Mersey Railway title worked into the stonework of the upper reaches of Birkenhead Central station still remained. "KEEP OFF CONDUCTOR RAILS" signs headed Mersey Railway could also be found here and there for long after the line was merged into British Railways. The most interesting survivals however, were the two windows in the handsome double doors at the entrance to the company's head office at Birkenhead Central station, each of which had an engraving of the Liver Bird crest. Unfortunately one window got broken, but the other one lasted intact, being removed and preserved. In 1982 the old offices were up for sale and the windows boarded over.

A larger and more solid reminder of the Mersey Railway might have been with us today in the shape of Car No.1 (B.R. No.28405) which was set aside for preservation in 1956. This car was hauled all the way to the carriage works at Derby and languished on a siding for some considerable time. At length, the car was moved into the works for overhaul and restoration to its original condition, but the very next day a blaze destroyed the carriage shop and a number of coaches, the old Mersey car among them — a sad stroke of misfortune indeed, for there were no other examples left. All the rest of the old rolling stock had been already disposed of, though one or two car bodies are believed to have been sold for use as pavilions on bowling greens etc.

Whilst the old Mersey Railway Company has vanished into the realm of history, its traditions of reliability and punctuality live on in the combined Mersey and Wirral lines that serve today's travellers with an efficiency that is the envy of passengers on some other lines in the Liverpool area, and bids fair to remain vital to the commerce of Merseyside for many years yet to come. Could the original promoters of the Mersey Railway return to the scene of their activities they would surely nod with satisfaction at the manner in which their railway performs its daily task of conveying legions of men, women and children on their errands of business and pleasure with scarcely an interruption — indeed, a stoppage on the Mersey lines is big news because of its rarity and the resultant inconvenience to the large numbers of passengers usually involved.

The new Loop Line platform at James Street, Liverpool. The train is bound for Rock Ferry. (Photo: G. Jones.)

James Street station, 1982. This view shows the former "inward" platform, now used only in emergencies. The existing "outward" platform, has been modernised and brilliantly illuminated, leaving the other platform in semi-darkness and drab condition. (Photo: G. Jones.)

Although the title Mersey Railway ceased to be applicable upon Nationalisation, it has been recently revived in slightly slicked-up form for the whole of the rail network of Liverpool, Birkenhead and district, all former local lines now being grouped under the collective title of MERSEYRAIL — a piece of inspired thinking put to good effect, for the name is exactly appropriate.

In Victorian times it was the custom to choose a motto for a business or other venture and endeavour to live up to it, this practice being followed by several railway companies. The one chosen by the Mersey Railway — "Shall Ride In Triumph Over All Mischance" turned out to be quite appropriate! These words must have been ingrained into the subconciousness of the people who controlled the company's affairs and ran the trains, for the line progressed from an almost penniless concern to one of comfortable prosperity, survived two World wars and the Railway Grouping, and although prosperity is not the lot of its successors, the old Mersey Railway tradition of efficiency lives on as much as possible in today's conditions. Indeed, there is little doubt that Major Isaac's railway will continue to play its part well in the new railway age, in which the suburban railway has seen a revival all over the World, following the lead of London, New York and now Merseyside, our own area having been the scene of so many milestones in railway progress.

ACKNOWLEDGEMENTS

The following sources were consulted in the preparation of this book: "A Few Facts About The Mersey Railway" (Mersey Railway Company): The Dictionary of National Biography; "The Engineer"; "The Railway Magazine"; "Railway World"; "Tramway and Railway World". Information on the new Loop Line is mainly from British Rail publicity.

For the supply of illustrations I am indebted to A.E. Astbury, H. Haddrill, J.B. Horne, K. Longbottom, Merseyside County Museums (via P. Rees), G. Jones, G.W. Rose and E. Shenton. The manuscript was typed by Patricia Shimmin. My thanks to all the above named for their assistance.

OTHER TITLES from COUNTYVISE and AVON ANGLIA

PUBLISHED JOINTLY:

Seventeen Stations to Dingle, by John W. Gahan. 88pp. A nostalgic history of the famous Liverpool Overhead Railway.
The Storeton Tramway, by R.C. Jermy. 64pp. A history of the quarry tramway in the Wirral, famed for the fact that the track used was that originally laid for the Liverpool to Manchester Railway.

PUBLISHED BY COUNTYVISE:

Ghost Ships of the Mersey, by K.J. Williams. 38pp. A brief history of Confederate cruisers with Mersey connections.
Companion to the Fylde, by R.K. Davies. 68pp. A history of the Fylde area of Lancashire. Easy to read style and many anecdotes to liven the text.
Sidelights on Tranmere, by J.E. Allison, M.A. 99pp. A masterly history of Tranmere, one of the oldest townships in the Wirral.
Speak through the Earthquake, Wind and Fire, by Graham A. Fisher. 155pp. This book adds a new viewpoint to the catastrophic theories propounded by Immanuel Velikovsky and Donald Patten.
Mersey Ferries. Illustrations by Ken Radcliffe. 32pp. Artists drawings and notes on Birkenhead and Wallasey Ferries.

PUBLISHED BY AVON ANGLIA:

Weston, Clevedon & Portishead Railway, by Christopher Redwood. A thorough, 184pp. illustrated hardback study of a light railway of character.
Heart of Wales Line. The history, route and operation of the line from Swansea and Llanelli to Shrewsbury. A5, 32pp.
Birmingham & Derby Junction Railway, by C.R. Clinker. A5, 24pp. The history of an early line that became part of an important trunk route.
Leicester & Swannington Railway, by C.R. Clinker. A detailed, 72pp. history bringing to life the origins of a pioneer Midlands railway.
Rocket 150 – The Liverpool & Manchester Railway 1830-1980, by Geoffrey Body. Both a comprehensive history of an important early railway and the official record produced for its 150th anniversary celebrations.
Ellesmere Port – Canal Town, by Adrian Jarvis. 44pp. The Shropshire Union Canal and the town it created.
Liverpool & Manchester: A Photographic Essay, by Geoffrey Body. The official photographic record of the 1980 Rainhill celebrations with full captions.
Railways on Record, by Jim Palm. 128pp. of data covering all known LP and 45 rpm records of British Railway sounds.
Rail Data Book, by I.G. Body. 32pp. of data on all aspects of BR.

Some general titles . . . . .

Rubaiyat of Omar Khayyam, Fitzgerald's first version printed on Glastonbury antique paper and with 12 coloured illustrations and 3 initials by Steven Morris.
Understanding French Cookery, a guide to French recipes and cooking terms.
The Hill of the Dragon, by Paul Newman. A fascinating 290pp., illustrated examination of dragon legends.
The Story of Hymns, by Doris Hodges. 128pp. hardback describing how many of our most popular hymns came to be written.

Being published in 1983 . . . . .

Northern Rail Heritage, by Ken Powell. A study of the great railway buildings and railway preservation in the counties of the North.